A Rebellious Faith

Cycle C Sermons
Based on Second Lessons for
Lent and Easter

Mark Ellingsen

CSS Publishing Company, Inc.
Lima, Ohio

A REBELLIOUS FAITH
CYCLE C SERMONS BASED ON SECOND LESSONS FOR
LENT AND EASTER

FIRST EDITION
Copyright © 2018
by CSS Publishing Co., Inc.

Library of Congress Cataloging-in-Publication Data
Names: Ellingsen, Mark, 1949- author.
Title: A rebellious faith : Cycle B sermons for Lent & Easter based on the second lesson texts / Mark Ellingsen.
Description: FIRST EDITION. | Lima : CSS Publishing Company, Inc., 2018. |
Includes bibliographical references and index.
Identifiers: LCCN 2018009492 (print) | LCCN 2018020809 (ebook) | ISBN 9780788029271 (Ebook) | ISBN 9780788029264 (pbk. : alk. paper)
Subjects: LCSH: Lenten sermons. | Eastertide--Sermons. | Bible. New Testament--Sermons. | Common lectionary (1992)
Classification: LCC BV4277 (ebook) | LCC BV4277 .E455 2018 (print) | DDC   252/.62--dc23

For more information about CSS Publishing Company resources, visit our website at www.csspub.com, email us at csr@csspub.com, or call (800) 241-4056.

e-book:
ISBN-13: 978-0-7880-2927-1
ISBN-10: 0-7880-2927-4

ISBN-13: 978-0-7880-2926-4
ISBN-10: 0-7880-2926-6

PRINTED IN USA

Contents

For our newest son
Jorge Santos
(and in memory of Cheryl and Jorge,
the great folks who raised him)

Foreword

Christians are odd people. They and their faith go against the grain. When the world says Sundays are for goofing off, for golf, shopping, or youth sports, Christians get up early and go off and worship. When the world busies itself in December with getting presents, Christians think more of giving (at least when they're doing their Christian thing). When the world readies itself for new life in spring, Christians first commemorate death (at Lent). When the world has its one-day Easter celebration (makes it a nice family day), Christians keep the celebration going six more weeks. Gee, Christians are an odd group (at least at our best we are).

I think that the problem mainline Christianity has been facing in its membership decline since the 1960's is that we have not been "strange" or "rebellious" enough. We have acted more like church-type (cultural) Christians who live a version of the faith in line with the powers that be. We practice a version of Christianity that makes it seem like the main qualification for faith is that you act like a good American, uphold traditional values and don't rock the boat much.[1] That version of faith is not very biblical, as the texts considered in this book will make clear. As a result, the sermons in this book, in trying to break with this too pervasive Christian model, will endeavor to rock the boat,

---

1   This vision of a Christianity, that is nothing more than the embodiment of the values of the elite, was nicely articulated by Ernst Troeltsch, *The Social Teachings of the Christian Churches, Vol.1* (New York: Macmillan, 1931), pp.331-337.

to present a version of the faith that goes against the grain. Hopefully these sermons will provide readers and those to whom they preach with some head-shaking, uncomfortable moments. In that case, to the degree that these sermons help shake things up in your congregation and community, go against the grain of American meritocracy, the Protestant Work Ethic, globalization, nationalism, be good to yourself, you don't need approval, you deserve what you have, and all the other "truths" that circulate today in pop culture, then I've really touched on the true meaning of Lent and Easter. Because, as we'll see, a lot of their ideas are down-right offensive to twenty-first-century ears!

As I've warned readers before in previous sermon books for CSS, don't use these sermons verbatim, preachers. They are written for the eye, and you need a manuscript that's written for the ear. It will not be hard to make adjustments and use these texts for your sermons. Just throw in more contractions, run some sentences together, or break them up when my sentences get too long. Repeat a few of the phrases you like sometimes for emphasis and indigenize the points for your congregation. Eliminate some of my analogies and insert stories or analogies that work better in your community. Make these sermons your own. Change them all you want. But don't change them so much that they stop going against the grain of what your hearers and the local town fathers/mothers believe. Be sure to let the Easter Word of grace have the final say over the Lenten demands for discipline and its word of judgment.

This book is dedicated to a rebel who goes against the grain — my son-in-law Jorge Santos. He may be an in-law, but in view of the joy he has brought our daughter and the wonderful young man that he is, to my wife Betsey and me he is really a third son. It is so neat to dedicate this book to him for several reasons. Over 25 years ago I dedicated a similar book in this series (Cycle A Sermons on the Gospels for Lent and Easter) — a book titled *Preparation and Manifestation* to his wife — our then four-year-old daughter Elizabeth! How fitting, then, that Jorge should get this one.

But he is the right man for this book for another reason. Like I noted, he goes against the grain. A member of the millennial generation who married before he was thirty, he is a faithful husband, doting father to our granddaughter, and a regular church-goer. What a counter-cultural rebel! He is a college graduate, who *wanted* to work with kids from tough backgrounds and a high-school coach (in his twenties) who likes teaching grade-schoolers. He embodies a lot of the counter-cultural Christianity I've been referring to. Of course Betsey and I can't take any credit for all our new son stands for. We didn't raise him. His deceased parents, Jorge Santos and Cheryl Gomez, with some help from his friend Ty Skinner's parents, Trudy and Billy, deserve those kudos, though Betsey and I are delighted to say he's ours too.

Ash Wednesday
2 Corinthians 5:20b — 6:10

The Hiddenness Of Life's Truths:
Christian Life As Surprise

The ashes of Ash Wednesday are icons proclaiming the hiddenness of God's ways. And God's ways are hidden. Paul tells us that in our lesson:

We are treated as imposters, and yet are true; as unknown, yet are well known; as dying, and see — we are alive; as punished, and yet not killed; as sorrowful, yet always rejoicing; as poor, yet making many rich; as having nothing, and yet possessing everything (6:8b-6:10).

It does not make sense, does it? How can we be imposters and yet the real thing, sorrowful but full of joy, poor but able to enrich others? Are you comfortable with these tensions in life? Why can't God simply will an end to death, sadness, suffering, and poverty, so we could live just ordinary American lives without all the hassles and confusion? What are we doing here on Ash Wednesday rubbing those ashes (the symbol of death) on our living bodies?

Our lesson gives us some answers for coming to terms with the paradoxes of Christian life, with why there are so many contradictions and ups and downs in life. Things don't turn out just the way we would like them, it seems, because of sin. In fact, Christ had to *become sin*, Paul says. That's how we got saved (5:20-5:21).

The nature of the good news of our faith is that we have a God who works in hidden ways. We see that in the Lenten season, how he brought life out of death. Martin Luther once explained the hidden ways of God forcefully:

And universally our every assertion of anything good is hidden under the denial of it, so that faith may have its place in God, who is a negative essence of goodness and wisdom and righteousness, who cannot be possessed or touched except by the negation of all our affirmatives.[2]

Christianity is full of paradoxes, because God is so great that he confounds all that we finite, sinful human beings can think and say about him.

But let's not forget that God has to work in hidden ways because he's had to work through evil in order to overcome sin. We can see this clearly tonight in the use of the ashes. These ashes (the symbol of death, because keep in mind that they were originally living things) get us back to life.

This also explains why there is still death, still sadness, and still suffering. In a hidden way God struggled with these realities. He may not have abolished them, but ultimately he is in control of them, and so he uses them to give life, joy, health, and to overcome poverty.

This sort of hidden working by God gets us to focus more on him. If we can come to realize, like we heard Martin Luther did, that all our wisdom is contradicted by God, then we have nowhere to turn except to the word of God. Get it? God's hiding himself helps us get

2   Martin Luther, "Lectures On Romans" (1515-1516), in *Luther's Works*, Vol.25 (63 vols.; St. Louis-Philadelphia: Concordia Publishing House-Fortress Press, 1955ff.), p.383.

ourselves out of the way. Since your latest great insight or thing you have done is just the opposite from truth, then Christians have to go against the grain. We wind up rejecting what the world wants us to act like and be. But we Christians know that the world's ways are all worthless. There's nowhere to turn for truth but to him — to Jesus!

Get the point? All the best things we do and think are flawed, all mired in sin — just ashes. That is the significance of this day. They remind us that all we do and are is leading us towards the grave. All we are and have done is filled with sin and so deserves death. All we do, even how we live as Christians, is marred by sin.

Martin Luther nicely elaborated further on these points:

> *You see the whole of Christian life has to be hidden and remain hidden in this way. It cannot achieve great fame or put on much of a display or show before the world. So let it go at that. Do not worry about the way it is hidden, covered up, and buried, and the way no one notices it. Be content with the fact that your Father up there notices. Be content with the fact that your Father up there in heaven sees it.*[3]

Or as he puts it in another context: A Christian is hidden from himself, "finding in ourselves nothing but sin, foolishness, death, and hell..."[4]

The Christian's life is hidden. That is what Paul is saying in our lesson. This confusion is what drives

---

3   Martin Luther, "The Sermon On the Mount" (1532 / 1534), in *Luther's Works*, Vol.21, pp.163-164.

4   Martin Luther, "The Heidelberg Disputation" (1518), in *Luther's Works*, Vol.31, pp.44.

us back to Christ. It's hidden because in all Christians do (even our good deeds) — it is marred by sin. They are all sin, because in everything we do we are selfish (concupiscent). Even our good deeds are done more for ourselves (they make us feel good about ourselves) than they are for God or the one we're helping. (See Romans 7:14-25.)[5]

Martin Luther brought together this paradoxical appreciation of how life looks life and should be lived from a Christian perspective. He called it "brave sinning":

> ... be not a false but a real [brave] sinner; not only in words but in reality and from the heart acknowledge yourself worthy before God of his wrath and eternal punishment, and bring before him in truth these words, "me a poor sinner."[6]

The next time you are uncertain of God's and Christ's presence in your life, be a brave sinner. Acknowledge that you sin in all you do, even in your seemingly good deeds. Do that, and you will realize that you have nowhere else to turn in everyday life, but to God and his grace. If anything good came out of what your did, you did not do it. It was a work of the Holy Spirit who took those mixed-motive, selfish deeds of yours and mine and made something good out of them.

5   Augustine, "On Marriage and Concupiscence" (419-420), in *Nicene and Post-Nicene Fathers, First Series, Vol.5*, trans. Robert Holmes and Robert Wallis (2nd print.; Peabody, MA: Hendrickson Publishers, 1995), pp.273-274.

6   Martin Luther, "Eleventh Sermon After Trinity, Second Sermon," in *The Complete Sermons of Martin Luther, Vol.2/2*, ed. John Lenker (Grand Rapids, MI: Baker Books, 2000), p.367.

See now how and why God's ways are hidden, why we can be imposters and still be the real thing, why in our poverty we can enrich others, why life overcomes death. We don't make it happen. We're too sinful, too selfish, to do any truly loving things (or good) on our own. It's just that God and his Holy Spirit take the flawed things we do and say and make good out of them.

Let that sink in. When you look at life in this way, in terms of how we're not capable of making things good, or helping others, of being joyful on our own, then you can't have the good things in life happen to you without seeing God in them. Because knowing how little you and I can do to make things good means that if they turn out good, it must have been God and the Spirit who did the good. The good in life is God's work. A radical, courageous affirmation of the truths of life, their hidden character, drives us into the arms of God.

There is another, related benefit that comes with appreciating the hidden character of God's ways. It entails that God works in surprising ways. That the good we have in life is surprising, just like it's a surprise that suffering can lead to joy, that defeat can lead to victory and that death can lead to life.

Surprise is what makes life beautiful. It's like Charlton Heston once said: "Life is full of surprises, isn't it?" Early twentieth-century Russian poet Boris Pasternak calls our attention to the joys of surprise: "Surprise [he wrote] is the great gift which life can grow." British-American anthropologist and humorist Ashley Motagu makes this point in even more depth with regard to the happiness of surprise: "The moments of happiness we enjoy take us by surprise, it is not that we seize them, but that they seize us."

Living with surprise and novelty, like the Christian who appreciates God's hidden ways, leads to happiness and pleasure. Surprising novelty seems to be good for the human brain and give us pleasure. Research conducted by neurologists has revealed that the pleasurable good-feeling brain chemical dopamine is secreted in the brain in greater quantities when the reward is greater than what was expected.[67]

The next time you encounter hard times and despair, the next time you wonder why there's so much lack of fairness in the world, wonder about God's ways, take a moment to reflect on the hidden character of the gospel. Confess your sin bravely. Remember the ashes you are receiving today. You and I deserve them. They epitomize the value of our lives without Jesus — just ashes blowing in the wind.

That way of thinking will get you ready, ready for Easter, ready for tomorrow. It can get us ready to look for the wonderful, surprising life that God has in store for us. The ashes of Ash Wednesday testify to God's wonderful, surprising ways of bringing life out of death, good out of bad and hope out of despair. He may have that planned for you this week, this year! Keep that hope alive, that trust in a loving God, and a lot of what's hidden in life will start to make sense to you.

---

7   Oscar Arrias-Carrion and Ernst Poppel, "Dopamine, learning, and reward-seeking behavior," *Acta Neruobiolae Experimentalis, Vol.67,* No.4 (2007): 481-488; cf. Stefan Klein, *The Science of Happiness,* trans. Stephen Lehmann (New York: Marlowe & Company, 2006), pp.35-37,56-58,107.

A Protestant (And Catholic) Way To Confess

Confession: Most Protestants are inclined to say that confession is Catholic and stop there. Or we hear it said, "Confession is good for the soul." Even then, we are likely to hear it like Roman Catholics[8], to suppose it means that we are to recount our sins. We don't need confession in our church! Or do we?

Paul gives us a model for confession of the faith in the Book of Romans. Recall that this book is a letter of introduction to the church in Rome. How does he make his introduction? With a confession of faith!

It is important to note here that Paul does not confess his sins in our lesson today. He begins by referring to the Word of faith (v.8b). Salvation, he says, comes as we confess that Jesus is Lord and believe that God raised him from the dead (v.9). One who believes is said to be justified, and one who confesses is saved (v.10). Citing Isaiah 28:16, Paul notes that no one who believes will be put to shame (v.11). No distinction between Jew and Gentile can be made, he adds. The Lord is lord of all and generous to all (v.12). Paul then cites Joel 2:32 (applying its reference of Yahweh to Jesus); he states that "everyone who calls on the name of the Lord will be saved" (v.13).

8   *Catechism of the Catholic Church* (Collegeville, MN: The Liturgical Press, 1994), 1456,1458.

We have other examples of Paul's version of confession in our other assigned Bible lessons. The first lesson includes a confession of faith of the Hebrews (in Deuteronomy 26:5-9). In the gospel, we hear Jesus confessing his faith (quoting scripture) in response to the devil's temptations (in Luke 4:4,8,12).

It is clear that confession in this biblical, catholic sense is about faith, the faith of the Church, not just the confession of sins. The Apostles' Creed and The Nicene Creed are examples of confessing faith like Paul, the Hebrews, and Jesus did. They are summaries of scripture. (Note: If the preacher is of a Lutheran or Reformed background she/he might note that the denominational founders in the Reformation era even formulated confessions, which to this day govern the teachings of the denomination.)

Just to recite the creeds (or the denominational catechisms) is not to be involved in confession. You and I only really confess when we know what we're saying and believe it. Keep that it mind the next time you recite the creed. The next time you have that chance, don't just recite it — *confess* it!

Certainly, confession needs to be in harmony with the whole church. If what you say is just your own private opinion, it is not a confession of faith you offer. An authentic confession of faith expresses the church's faith! This is such an appropriate concern for us to consider here at the beginning of Lent. Because in its origin, Lent was a period of instruction in what the church believed, so that those being baptized on Easter (the day of Baptism in the early church) would adequately be prepared to confess the faith on that day.[9]

9   See Luther Reed, *The Lutheran Liturgy* (4th print.; Philadelphia: Fortress, 1975), p.492.

We need this kind of confession of the church's faith especially today. We need it to counter the loneliness and self-serving individualism which is growing in America today. We are living in a world in which a sense of loneliness is growing in America (especially since the 1980's). A 2016 Harris poll indicated that 72% of us say that we are lonely.[10] We even do our religion more and more on our own. That's why although the number of Americans not religiously affiliated is growing (23% according to the Pew Research Center), 9 in 10 Americans still believe in God (Gallup polls report).[11] A number of social analysts think that this a function of the new American way of doing business in America, the demand for flexibility, reinvention, and openness to change. The point is that with this new set of management mantras, there is no "long term." And no long term corrodes trust, loyalty, and commitment. But strong ties, by contrast, depend on trust and long association. As business undermines these values, it is only natural that the message to the labor force is that "you're on your own." That's precisely the message and value system you take into your personal life too. Add to that that the millennial generation has been raised with the ethic of putting yourself first and being good to yourself, and you can understand why so many of us are inclined to go our own way, to go it alone when others are tying you down.[12]

10   Other relevant data is found in Dihruu Khulla, "How Social Isolation Is Killing Us," *The New York Times* (December 22, 2016).

11   See Jean Twenge, *Generation Me: Why Today's Young Americans Are More Confident, Assertive, Entitled — and More Miserable Than Ever Before* (New York and London: Free Press, 2006), pp.34-36.

12   Richard Sennett, *The Corrosion of Character: The Personal Consequences of Work in the New Capitalism* (New York and London: W. W. Norton, 1998), esp. pp.24ff.; Twenge, pp.4ff.

No doubt, we need an antidote to the rampant "do it my way" ethos of today. Confession is that antidote. For when you confess, you are confessing not just your faith, but the faith of your fellow-members, the faith of all your deceased Christian ancestors, the faith your great-great grandchildren (God-willing) will have, the faith of this congregation's charter members, the faith of our denomination's founders, the faith of the first followers of Jesus. You don't stand alone when you confess the faith!

An authentic confession of faith gets you and me away from the loneliness and self-serving individualism of our day, because you're confessing not just your faith, but the faith all those before you and those to come. A communal confession unites us together in a way that can critique all these individualistic trends.

Another by-product of our loneliness and individualism seems to be that we do not trust each other much, especially not our leaders. You know the numbers. As recently as 2017, Gallup found only 18% of us really trust lawyers (business leaders not much higher), members of Congress 6%, less than 1 in 2 Americans trust clergy (44%), and cops only have a 58% trust level. As we confess together over the years we come to feel that we are kin in hearts and minds. We come to trust each other. (I also am more likely to forget about myself, as I come to focus more on the content of my confession and on these who share that confession.) The result: social solidarity! The walls of suspicion start tumbling down when you share a common faith, or at least when your neighbor has the same job as someone with whom you share a common faith and trust.

The other-directed dimensions of confession promote more activity in the front part of our brains (the prefrontal cortex). It seems that when that happens it stimulates the secretion of the amphetamine-like pleasurable brain chemical dopamine. As we've noted previously, dopamine feels good.[13]Confession is good for the church, good for society, and nurtures happy believers. That happiness, that joy, even gets better when you realize what it is we Christians confess, what Paul confessed.

Paul makes clear that his confession is about justification by grace through faith (vv.10,13). What we do, our works, are not what determines whether you are saved. Martin Luther made this so clear:

It follows, then, that a Christian must not believe that we are justified by an other righteousness. Let all works by which we aim to gain righteousness and all our own merits depart, because we are built upon the foundation not by doing works but by believing. Therefore let every godly man terrified by sin run to Christ as the mediator and propitiator, and let him leave all his own works behind.[14]

What all this implies, Luther went on to say, is that

Believing in him [Christ] is the thing. It is useful and gives the power that we have from this: that neither hell nor the devil can take us and all others who believe him captive nor can they do us harm.[15]

13   Dean Hamer, *The God Gene* (New York: Anchor Books, 2004), pp.72ff.; Anthony Walsh, *The Science of Love* (Amherst, NY: Prometheus Books, 1996).

14   Martin Luther, "Lectures On Isaiah" (1527-1530), in *Luther's Works, Vol. 16* (63 vols.; St. Louis-Philadelphia: Concordia Publishing House-Fortress Press, 1955ff.), pp.230-231.

15   Martin Luther, *Torgau Sermon On Christ's Descent into Hell and the Resurrection* (1533), in *Sources and Contexts of The Book of Concord*, eds. Robert Kolb and James A. Nestingen (Minneapolis: Fortress, 2001), p.249.

We can, John Calvin once said, "rest with a sweet confidence in God..."[16]

The focus on the grace of God and that that is the only way we're saved defines what confession is. At least that is what the famous ancient African theologian (a great influence on the first Protestants and Catholicism's number one theologian to this day) Saint Augustine thought. He wrote a book called "The Confessions." Here is how he defined confession:

> For when I am wicked confession to You [O Lord] means being displeased with myself; but when I am good, confession to you means simply not attributing any goodness to myself.[17]

Both Saint Patrick and Martin Luther said something like this too. First Patrick:

> So now I commend my soul to you my most trustworthy God on whose behalf I am carrying out a mission, for all my humble status, but because he has no respect for persons he has even chosen me for this post that I should be among his lowest servants.[18]

And then Luther adds:

> For confession is the principal work of faith by which as man denies himself and confesses God and thus he both denies and confessed to such an extent that he would

16   John Calvin, Commentary On The Book of Psalms (1563), in Calvin's Commentaries, Vol. V/2, trans. James Anderson (Grand Rapids, MI: Baker Books, 2005), p.489.

17   Augustine, Confessions (397), in Nicene and Post-Nicene Fathers, First Series, Vol.1, ed. Philip Schaff (2nd print.; Peabody, MA: Hendrickson Publishers, 1995), p.142.

18   Patrick, The Confession, in The Life and Writings of the Historical Saint Patrick, 56, trans. R. P. C. Hanson (New York: Seabury, 1983), p.120.

deny his own life and all things rather than affirm him-
self. For in confessing God and denying himself he dies.[19]

Confession is about not attributing too much to yourself and giving all the credit to God!

To confess the faith in this Protestant/Catholic
way gives confidence and joy. Temptation and despair
don't have a chance when we have renounced our own
goodness. A confessor of the faith does not face the
problems of life alone, and so he or she does not even
have to be the one to fight these traits. When you are
a confessor, the whole Body of Christ and God himself
in the Holy Spirit is right there with you to stand up to
all the evil. A confession of faith reminds us that we are
totally dependent on God, and that he will take care of
all our problems. Against that, temptation and despair
are bound to wither away! Meet your trials this week
with a confessed faith. And yes in the big picture of life
they will all wither away, for collectively and in face of
God — they ultimately have no chance.

19   Martin Luther, "Lectures On Romans" (1515-1516), in *Luther's Works*,
      Vol.25, p.411.

Lent 2
Philippians 3:17 — 4:1

Hanging Around Jesus Changes You

Writing to Christians in a Macedonian city of Philippi, Paul writes: "For many live as enemies of the cross of Christ..." (v.18). People don't like this message, don't want anything to do with the cross of Christ. No surprise. Who of us wants to mess with death and suffering? Why, it's just common sense.

Cross-bearing goes against the grain of what pop culture in America tells us about life. It goes against the grain of our desire for instant gratification. After all, we've been taught to follow our dreams, to let nothing get in the way of personal goals.[20] This is what the prosperity gospel of today is all about.

We want prosperity because things are not that good in America today. A CNN/Money e-Trade 2016 poll found that more than half of us (56%) think things will be worse in America for our children. The Anxiety and Depression Association of America reports that nearly 1 in 5 of us (18%) is depressed. Economically it is harder and harder to maintain a middle-class lifestyle, and more and more America is becoming an aging nation. In the 2017 World Happiness Report, the US ranked nineteenth, down from third in a decade.

---

20   This characterization of American life, especially for the Millennial generation has been offered by Jean Twenge, *Generation Me: Why Today's Young Americans Are More Confident, Assertive, Entitled — and More Miserable Than Ever Before.*

No doubt a number of these problems have been occasioned by our desires to live as enemies of Christ, to make our bellies into our god (3:18-19). A National Survey of Family Growth report indicated that in the 2010's only 5% of brides were virgins. Sociologist Paula England found 28% of college women hooked up more than ten times in their years of matriculation. The US Census Bureau has found that the average U.S. home is 1,000 square feet bigger than the 1973 average home. We can't afford it. CNBC reported that in 2016, the average American household had $16,000 in credit-card debt.

Lent is a time for coming to terms with our unfaithfulness, without our waywardness and love for our bellies. This is why you and I need to hear the word of condemnation that Paul delivers in this lesson. Martin Luther was preaching a sermon on this text and made a similar point:

The world cannot conduct itself in any other way, when the declaration comes from heaven saying: "True you are a holy man, a great and learned jurist... and honorable citizen, and so on, but with all our authority and your upright character you are going to hell; your every act is offensive and condemned in God's sight. If you would be saved you must become an altogether different man; your mind and heart must be changed.[21]

The best of us deserve hell. We need to become different people, need a total change of heart and mind.

John Calvin made similar points; and so he once wrote:

21   Martin Luther, "Sermon for Twenty-Third Sunday After Trinity," in *The Complete Sermons of Martin Luther*, Vol.4/2, ed. John Lenker.

For such is the viciousness of our nature, that the more we are taught what is right and just, the more openly is our iniquity discovered.[22]

Paul has good news for the Philippians and us. He says that Christ is coming to transform us, so that we may be conformed to his body (3:21). Hanging around Christ changes you! It leads you to take up Jesus' cross.

Acknowledging our sin, denying our goodness, is a kind of cross to bear. It doesn't *feel* good. But Paul and the gospel say that it *is* good for us. Crosses in life make us all the more dependent on God's love. It is like the seventeenth-century Scottish clergyman Samuel Rutherford once put it: "How soon would faith freeze without a cross."

Again John Calvin put it nicely:

... when we are called by the Lord we emerge from nothing; for whatever we seem to be we have not, no not a spark of anything good which can render us fit for the kingdom of God that we may indeed on the other hand be in a suitable state to hear the call of God, we must be altogether dead in ourselves.[23]

When called by Christ we emerge from nothing. Around Jesus, nobodies become somebodies.

Think about this. If you're somebody, you don't need that bigger house to convince yourself you've made it. You already have it made with God. If you're already somebody, you do not need the latest must-have gadget that you cannot afford.

Martin Luther had it right. We can be certain and confident, he said, because we are snatched outside

22 John Calvin, "Commentaries On The Epistle of Paul the Apostle To the Romans" (1539), in *Calvin's Commentaries*, Vol. XIX/2, trans. James Anderson.

23 Ibid., p.175.

ourselves, so we don't need to depend on ourselves, our strength, conscience, experience, person or works, and can depend on God, on the righteousness He gives us, which is a lot more certain than we could ever be in ourselves.[24] Again, we see how faith makes nobodies into somebodies.

Faith in Christ, hanging around Jesus, changes you. It makes a difference in how you live your life. Martin Luther offers some deep insights on this matter:

> *Faith is divine work in us, which changes us and makes us be born anew of God... O, it is a living, busy, active mighty thing this faith. It is impossible for it not to be doing good works incessantly... This knowledge of and confidence in God's grace [that faith provides] makes men glad and bold and happy in dealing with God and with all creatures. And this is the work that the Holy Spirit performs in faith. Because of it, without compulsion, a person is ready and glad to do good to everyone, to serve everyone, to suffer everything out of love and praise to God who has shown him grace.[25]*

Faith changes you, like a marriage or any intimate human bond you have ever had changes you. The famed medieval mystic Bernard of Clairvaux made this clear. He once wrote:

> *When God loves, he seeks nothing but love in return... knowing that those who love him become by that love itself most blessed... Therefore it is that he is a bridegroom*

24   Martin Luther, "Lectures On Romans" (1515-1516), in *Luther's Works*, Vol. 25, p.387.

25   Martin Luther, "Preface to the Epistle of St. Paul to the Romans" (1546/1522), in *Luther's Works*, Vol.35, pp.370-371.

and the soul is a bride, for this belongs only to a wedded pair.[26]

Give more thought to that image. Couples, is it not true that you are not the same since you met or since the wedding day? And has not a lot of your lover rubbed off on you? Hasn't your mate taken on a lot of your ways of doing things? Living together in love changes you, makes you more like your lover. And that does not happen by imitation or design. It just seems to happen without your thinking about it. It just somehow mysteriously happens.

It is the same with a parent-child relationship. Those of us who are parents, from the first time you laid eyes on that child of yours it changed you, did it not? And in a close relationship, as that child becomes an adult, whose values you admire, is it not true you can learn from that child, that his or her ways of looking at the world become yours? Not that you self-consciously try to imitate your child's outlook. It is just that it seems to happen, probably because the adult child loved you enough to share that part of him or her, and you love the child enough to admire him or her.

Look at yourself, those of you with a warm relationship with a parent or a grandparent: Are you not a chip off the old block? I see that a lot in myself — as I am my father with planning ahead and looking at every problem in life with a feeling that it can be solved with planning and logic. Or I'm my mother when I am breaking ice in a conversation by asking people about themselves. We never consciously try to imitate who our parents are. It's true that we share their gene pool,

26 Bernard of Clarivaux, in *Varieties of Mystic Experience*, ed. Elmer O'Brien (New York: Rinehart & Winston, 1964), p.104.

but we are different. It's just that the love we have for them, their love for us, changes our lives. If it can happen with human love, think how an all-powerful divine love can change you.

No two ways about it. America needs to be changed in order to get out of all the messes in which we find ourselves — all the pessimism, Narcissistic quest for fulfillment, the lack of long-term commitment.[27] Hanging around Jesus does it for us, transforms us into folks not willing to fall prey to the ways of the world, confident and secure enough to live with joy and the good of others. Remember, getting intimate with Jesus means taking on his thing, his agendas. One of them is bearing a cross, saying "no" to yourself for the sake of others. Jesus did that on Good Friday, with his whole life, and now that heritage is yours and mine in faith. And since bearing the cross is now who we are it's a little easier for Christians to say "no" to all the things pop culture says we should do and want.

Yes, hanging around Jesus changes you. But be careful: All that self-denial and saying "no" to instant gratification will make you down-right subversive, a party-pooper. Why someone who is a joyful cross-bearer is likely to be bad for the American economy — won't buy as much and be as flexible in relationships as our economy wants the worker to be. Yes, hanging around Jesus transforms you and me into the kind of person who goes against the grain.

---

27 For how the economy encourages these values, see Richard Sennett, *The Corrosion of Character: The Personal Consequences of Work in the New Capitalism* (New York and London: W. W. Norton, 1998), esp. pp.24ff.

Lent 3
1 Corinthians 10:1-13

Nobody's Too Good To Repent"

Historically, dating back to ancient times, the third Sunday in Lent was the time when candidates for baptism on Easter (the day when the ancient church performed all baptisms) were given careful scrutiny regarding how prepared they were to become followers of Jesus.

In Latin it was called *Occuli* [Eyes] Sunday, because it was the Sunday that the church had its eye on those who were to be baptized.[28] If we want to keep in touch with this heritage, this is a Sunday, then, for us to reflect how we have been doing as Christians and to vow to change as we fall short.

The second lesson for today gives us some clues for evaluating ourselves on the question of how we are doing as Christians. You won't want to hear the answer. How are we doing as Christians? Paul says: Not very well. Let's review what he said.

Paul says in our lesson that the ancient Hebrews sinned, even though they had received signs of God's love, just like we Christians have to this day (vv.3-6). If the devoted followers of Moses sinned, people who had trusted God enough to leave their Egyptian homeland, if they sinned, is it any surprise that we are sinners too?

28 See Luther Reed, *The Lutheran Liturgy* (4th print.; Philadelphia: Fortress, 1975), p.494.

Let's take a look first at how we 21st Americans are guilty on the very issues Paul warned — idolatry and sexual immorality (vv.7-8). One poll taken early in the decade estimated that if you count internet affairs, 50% of married women and 60% of married men have engaged in extramarital affairs. A 2017 Gallup Poll stated that 73% of the Americans deem divorce morally acceptable, 69% find extra-marital sex morally acceptable, and 62% see nothing wrong with out-of-wedlock birth.

How about idolatry? If free sex is not a false god, how about materialism, the latest goods?

In the most recent study on the subject (in 2016) it was found that our shopping mania had led to household debt that exceeds disposable income by 105%! We will do anything, it seems, even jeopardize our futures or our children's educations in order to serve the gods of materialism.

"Oh come on, Pastor. You are much too judgmental. This is just innocent shopping. It's the American way." That's the point. We really think we are good — too good to need repentance. But that's not how Paul sees it in this lesson (or most anything else he writes).

There is no way that you and I (or any human being) can avoid the concerns raised, even those of us not caught up in materialism and sexual license. Martin Luther once (all too clearly) explained why:

The reason is that our nature has been so deeply curved in upon itself because of the viciousness of original sin that it not only turns the finest gifts of God in upon itself and enjoys them (as is evident in the case of legalists and hypocrites), and indeed it even uses God Himself to achieve these aims, but it also seems to be ignorant of the very fact that in acting so iniquitously, so perversely, and in such a depraved way, it is even seeking God for its own sake.[29]

We are always trying to get our own way in everything we do. We're inherently selfish since the fall into sin and that selfishness infects even our good deeds.

Think about it: Have you ever done a deed that was not motivated at least in part by a desire to feel good about it? Is that not the reason we do good, because the deed makes us feel good about ourselves? I know my good deeds, raising kids, loving my wife Betsey, caring for students or for the poor seem selfless, until you scratch me deep enough, and see all the goodies I get out of them.

This selfishness infecting our outwardly good deeds means that what we do is not done in self-giving agape love. And that is what makes all we do sin. Research on the human brain supports this understanding. When you do good or practice spirituality your brain is flooded with a pleasurable brain chemical, dopamine, which has properties of amphetamines.[30] In fact, love and prayer feel good. On this side of the fall into sin, our prayers and caring for others are selfish deeds, make us feel good and may be at least sub-consciously motivated by the desire to feel good. You and I need to repent of our selfishness.

The health of your faith depends on recognizing these realities. John Calvin noted powerfully the misery in which we find ourselves:

29 Martin Luther, "Lectures On Romans" (1515-1516), in *Luther's Works*, Vol.25 (63 vols.; St. Louis-Philadelphia: Concordia Publishing House-Fortress Press, 1955ff.), p.291.

30 Dean Hamer, *The God Gene*, pp.72ff.; Anthony Walsh, *The Science of Love*.

*Those who are puffed up with vain confidence and are
satiated, or who, intoxicated by earthly appetites do not
feel thirst or soul, will not receive Christ.*[31]

No two ways about it. We need to repent. It's like
the ancient African theologian Clement of Alexandria
once said: "For unless a man believes that to which he
was addicted to be sin, he will not abandon it..."[32]

Repentance is nothing more than a hatred of sin,
not liking where we are headed with our selfishness
and acquisitiveness. That's all God wants. And the
good news is that we don't even have to do it. God's
love, God's grace, does it for us. Pope Benedict XVI
spoke profoundly on this matter, on how any change
in our lives is the result of grace:

*He [God] has loved us first, and he continues to do so; we
too, then, can respond with love... He loves us, he makes
us see and experience his love, and since he has "loved
us first," love can also blossom as a response within us.*[33]

And Clement of Alexandria, whom we met earlier, also
insisted that repentance is just an effect of faith.[34]

What happens to you when sin is renounced in this
way? It does not make you perfect.[35] It does not mean

31   John Calvin, "Commentary On the Book of the Prophet Isaiah"
      (1550), in *Calvin's Commentaries, Vol. VIII/2*, trans. James Anderson
      (Grand Rapids, MI: Baker Books, 2005), p.156.

32   Clement of Alexandria, "The Stomata" (194), in *Ante-Nicene Fathers,
      Vol.2*, eds. Alexander Roberts and James Donaldson (2nd print.; Pea-
      body, MA: Hendrickson, 1995), p.353.

33   Benedict XVI, *God Is Love* (Vatican: Ignatius Press, 2006), pp.42-43.

34   Clement of Alexandria, p.353.

35   Holiness/Methodist users of the sermon might revise this point,
      noting that perfection is linked to an appreciation of renouncing
      sin such that the faithful do not want to sin any more. See *The Book
      of Discipline of The United Methodist Church* (Nashville, TN: United
      Methodist Publishing, 2004), p.47.

that there will not still be temptations, that all the self-ishness and materialism will vanish (v.13). Famed modern theologian (a martyr in the persecutions by Hitler of his opponents) Dietrich Bonhoeffer described the outcome of repentance in a profound way. He wrote:

Let us leave this... repentance worship service not with despondent hearts, but with joyous and believing hearts. Come judgment day — joyfully we wait for you since we shall see the merciful Lord and take his hand and he will love us.[36]

Repentance leads to joy, because we know that God is taking us in his hand to change us, even if not every problem is solved. The Scottish Reformer John Knox told the brethren that for those in Christ all troubles are tolerable.[37] When you know you are in God's hand, everything is tolerable.

Have you been wondering how you are doing in your walk with God? Uncertain if you have the strength to withstand the temptations and the tough things in life? There is good news. We have a God who is there to take each of us in his hand, a God who will turn you around and will never let you and me go! Nobody's too good to repent. And nobody's so far gone that God will not be there to turn her or him around.

36 Dietrich Bonhoeffer, "On Repentance" (1933), in *A Testament of Hope*, eds. Geffrey B. Kelly and F. Burton Nelson (New York: Harper San Francisco, 1990), p.230.

37 John Knox, "An Exposition of The Sixth Psalm of David" (1580), in *The Works of John Knox*, Vol.3, ed. David Laing (Edinburgh: Bannatyne Club, 1854), p.125.

Lent 4
2 Corinthians 5:16-21

A New Beginning

Is it really possible to make a fresh start? Can you really have a new beginning in relationships or on the job? Are new beginnings really possible?

Normally the answer to these questions is "no." Bad marriages and bad parent-child relationships do not usually get better. And once institutions get established they resist change. We are pretty dull, monotonous people!

Part of the reason that change is so difficult is because we have histories that shape us and our character. We are the sum total of what we have done or the choices we have made. Famed New Testament scholar Rudolf Bultmann nicely made this point:

The Christian conception of the human being is that man is essentially a temporal being, which means that he is an historical being, who has a past which shapes his character...[38]

Yes, the past is who we are, but we are not totally satisfied with the way things have happened in life. We wish things were different, better.

Americans still have hope (sort of). Our feel-good, therapeutic ethos and its media gurus say it is possible, especially if we buy the right products, network

38   Rudolf Bultmann, *Jesus Christ and Mythology* (New York: Charles Scribner's Sons, 1958), p.30.

with enough important people, and make wise invest-ments.[39] But what we do will not provide this sort of security for which we yearn. In line with Paul's warning in Romans 7:18b-19 that we are trapped by our past and cannot do what we wish we could do, Rudolf Bultmann explains why we need a new beginning, but can't make it happen on our own:

> ... *man forgets in his selfishness and presumption....* *that it is an illusion to suppose that real security can be* *gained by men organizing their own personal and com-* *munity life. There are encounters and destinies which* *man cannot master. He cannot secure endurance for his* *works. His life is fleeting and its end is death. History* *goes on and pulls down all the towers of Babel again and* *again. There is no real, definitive security, and it is pre-* *cisely this illusion to which men are prone to succumb in* *their yearning for security.*[40]

Self-improvement will not alleviate our predicament.

We want meaning and security in life. But all that we might accumulate will not provide this, do not really change us. And so we remain the same insecure, uncertain, boring, or too cocky and selfish jerks we always were. Besides, all we possess or accomplish will wither and die. We are all on the way to the grave.

You and I want to forget these harsh realities, but it is good to be reminded of our dire circumstances during Lent. This is a season of repentance, as we have noted. Yet all the repenting in the world that you and I

39 For a similar characterization of American society offered two decades ago, but still relevant, see Christopher Lasch, *The Revolt of the Elites and the Betrayal of Democracy* (New York and London: W. W. Norton, 1995) esp. pp.6-7,29-30,40-41.

40 Rudolf Bultmann, *Jesus Christ and Mythology* (New York: Charles Scribner's Sons, 1958), pp.39-40.

try to do cannot change our circumstances and will not in itself make us new. John Calvin made a fine point in this connection. He once wrote:

> It is wretched sophistry to infer from this, that the grace of God is not exhibited to sinners until they anticipate it by their repentance... it is wrong to infer from this, that repentance, which is the gift of God is yielded by men from their own movement of their hearts.[41]

We can only have a new beginning, repentance only really happens, if God gives it to us. He did that on the first Easter!

In our lesson (v.17) Paul made this point about the new beginning we now have. But how can this be if you are stuck in a dead-end job, a failing marriage, have a bad child, or a bad reputation in school? How could you lie to us, Paul, like you seem to be in this lesson? How can we get this fresh start?

Lent and Easter are times for us to confess our sin and disbelief and to confess how we have squandered all the new opportunities Jesus has given us. We have missed how God has changed us. This word was at the heart of Jesus' preaching of the kingdom of God coming near (Mark 1:5 — a text that most historians agree is one of the most ancient, historically accurate accounts of Jesus' preaching and teaching). Repent and believe that the new has come and that the past no longer holds us in chains.

This message is evident in our other two lessons today. We see it in the first lesson's proclamation that the Hebrews are no longer slaves (Joshua 5:9). It also

---

41 John Calvin, "Commentary On a Harmony of the Evangelists, Matthew, Mark, and Luke" (1555), in *Calvin's Commentaries, Vol. XVI/2*, trans. James Anderson (Grand Rapids, MI: Baker Books, 2005), p. 347.

reflects in the gospel lesson's account of the prodigal son. His father gave him a fresh start (Luke 5:11b-32). When you hang around Jesus, new beginnings, improved relationships, and more fulfilling ways of life just seem to happen. We see this word in the second lesson, with its word that we are not to regard anyone from a human point of view (v.16a). Anyone in Christ is proclaimed to be a new creation. The old has passed (v.17)! This new beginning is a glimpse of the end tmes.

This new beginning is the result of the fact that Christ has reconciled us to God, forgiven us for how we've been lousing up our lives to date (vv.18-19). And it's like anti-Apartheid leader Bishop Desmond Tutu once said: "Forgiveness says you are given another chance to make a new beginning."

New beginnings, fresh starts, really are possible from God's point of view. Lent is a season for helping us see that this is possible. Yes, Lent is an unattractive time, filled with sobriety. Yet it opens the way to the Easter celebration. It is God's style to do things in surprising ways. That is what Paul means by calling us not to look at things from a human point of view (v.16a).

Don't look at things from a human point of view, because we are in a new time. God clearly does not do things our way and does not work in accord with our expectations. The way in which our Lord loves and forgives makes that apparent. The great reformed theologian of the last century, Karl Barth, profoundly explains the nature of God's forgiveness in this text. He wrote:

> The act of divine forgiveness is that God sees and knows
> this stain [of human sin] infinitely better than man him-

self and abhors it. He covers it. He passes it by, he puts it behind him, he does not charge it to man.[42]

Martin Luther also nicely explains the sense in which we should not look at things from a human point of view. For God's love does not operate as we would expect love to work. The message of the cross, Luther says, is that while human love comes into being through that which is pleasing to it, "the love of God does not find, but creates that which is pleasing to it."[43]

God has put the past behind us. He does not love like human love works. God loves the kind of person he is going to make us to be. Not *what is* but what *will be* is what he loves.

John Wesley nicely described what this new life in Christ looks like, how we live with our new beginning. He wrote:

He [the Christian] has new life, new senses, new faculties, new affections, new appetites, new ideas and conceptions. His whole tenor of action and conversation is new, and he lives, as it were, in a new world. God, men, the whole creation, heaven, earth, and all therein appear in a new light and stand related to Him in a new manner since he was created anew in Christ Jesus.[44]

People made new in that sense can do what medieval mystic Meister Eckhart once suggested: "Be willing to be a beginner every single morning."

42   Karl Barth, *Church Dogmatics*, Vol.IV/1, trams. G. W. Bromiley (Edinburgh: T. & T. Clark, 1956), p.597.

43   Martin Luther, "The Heidelberg Disputation" (1518), in *Luther's Works*, Vol.31, p.41.

44   John Wesley, *Commentary On the Bible* (Grand Rapids, MI: Francis Asbury Press, 1990), p.525.

Do you feel dead and need a new beginning? There is much to celebrate this day. You have a fresh start thanks to Jesus! It is a matter of looking at life, looking at the people in our lives, like God does. It's time for you and me to stop being hung up on what looks pleasing, on what looks good. The new beginning that Paul and Jesus promise gets you to see things differently. Even age and circumstances can't bind you anymore. God's fresh start means we can live life as famed Christian writer C. S. Lewis advised: "You are never too old to set another goal or dream a new dream.." The unattractive ways of God and his creatures really are beautiful. No matter what the world says, life is beautiful too. Christians do indeed go against the grain, and rebel against the world and its ways.

Lent 5
Philippians 3:4b-14

Giving It All Up For Jesus And What's Ahead

Take a moment to consider all you have done with your life. Whatever you came up with, Paul says in our lesson that it's just the past. We ought to look at the past like twentieth-century American poet Paul Eldridge once wrote: "Praises for our past triumphs are as feathers to a dead bird." Get over your successes. No matter how good you have been, how spiritual you are, no matter how much you have accomplished, it does not matter.

We Americans do not want to hear this. Think of Marvin and Harriet Thompson. (*Substitute the name accordingly and locate them age-wise, economically, and vocationally in accord with the prevailing demographics of your congregation.*) They are successfully situated in our community, with good reputations and even influence in the community. They are proud of their accomplishments.

Americans in general have these feelings about themselves. A 2017 Wall Street Journal NBC News poll found that 60% of Americans are optimistic. A 2016 LifeWay poll found that 65% of us think we are good. This is probably related to the fact that the majority of Americans do not accept a necessary role for grace in saving us. The most recent poll on the subject (in 2005 by the Barna Research Group) found that more than half of Americans (54%) think that people who are good *earn* salvation.

Do you know what Paul says to all this and to us regarding these and all our accomplishments? All we have been and done in the past is rubbish (v.8)! How can that be? Marvin and Harriet have lots to be proud of. Their success (our success), their good reputation (our good reputation) can't be rubbish!

Why is what we have done rubbish? Famed New Testament scholar Rudolf Bultmann nicely explains why we need to get free from our past and why it is sinful. We come into every new situation, he claimed, as the people we are through our previous decisions. But that suggests that our decisions are not really free but are determined by our past decisions. Truly to be free, you and I need to be free of our past.[45] And we can't get free on our own, because we are in bondage to selfishness and sin.

Selfishness: It is the essence of sin, according to Saint Augustine (and Saint Paul). We are so hung up on ourselves that everything we do is done for selfish reasons. Augustine called this concupiscence.[46] Think it over yourself. Concupiscence is a term that ordinarily refers to a strong or abnormal desire, especially in sex. This desire is what sin is all about. I want what you have, so I kill or steal. I want your good reputation, so I pull you down with lies. Augustine and Paul (the Protestant Reformers too) said you have this desire even

---

45 Rudolf Bultmann, *History and Eschatology: The Presence of Eternity* (New York: Harper & Row, 1957), p.44.

46 Augustine, "On Marriage and Concupiscence" (419-420), in *Nicene and Post-Nicene Fathers*, First Series, Vol.5, ed. Philip Schaff, pp.273-274.

when you do good deeds.[47]

That's why you and I do good. It feels good; we take bows for our goodness. In close relationships in which we make sacrifices for our partner, we get goodies out of the relationship. Even child-rearing works that way. Sure you make a lot of sacrifices for your children, but when they succeed while still under your roof, and when they turn out good as adults, it give you a lot of occasions to pat yourself on the back, even to get your (un)fair share of compliments. (Unfair, because it was really the child [by the grace of God], not you, who did the good things.)

Oh, how we use our friends, lovers, and children. This is why all we have been and done is rubbish (v.8). John Calvin made this point very clearly:

Paul, however, condemns here such looking back, as either destroys or impairs alacrity. Thus, for example, should anyone persuade himself that he has made sufficiently great progress, reckoning that he has done enough, he will become indolent... or, if any one looks back with a feeling of regret for the situation that he has abandoned, he cannot apply the whole bent of his mind to what he is engaged in.[48]

It is essential that we not get preoccupied with our-selves, or we will take our focus off Christ!

47 Philip Melanchthon, "Apology of The Augsburg Confession" (1531), in *The Book of Concord*, eds. Robert Kolb and Timothy J. Wengert (Minneapolis: Fortress Press, 2000), p.116; John Calvin, *Institutes of the Christian Religion*, Vol.1, ed. John McNeill (2 vols; Philadelphia: Westminster, 1960), p.296.

48 John Calvin, "Commentaries On the Epistle of Paul To the Gala-tians" (1548), in *Calvin's Commentaries*, Vol. XXI/2, trans. James An-derson, p.102.

The answer to all this? When you give yourself up, you wind up having your focus on Christ, and that changes you.

Jesus won't let us go. He will not reject us! A famous preacher of the first centuries, John Chysostom (his name means John the "golden-mouthed one") explained nicely how God has made us his own:

> ... He [God] saw us in such great guilt, he did not reject us; was not wroth, turned not away, hated us not, for he was a master, and could not hate his own creation.[49]

Christ sets us free from the need to justify our own existence and righteousness, based on what we have accomplished. That righteousness is nothing but bull! Again John the golden-mouthed one was right on the money. He compared the law by which we are supposed to abide to waste, but noted that waste has a use as from it wheat is gathered.[50] And in its place, in place of the righteousness we think we achieve by being good, God instead gives us his own righteousness through Christ!

Since we have nothing left but Christ, now that we know that what we bring to the table is useless waste, Paul speaks of how we Christians yearn to know Christ and the power of his Resurrection, the sharing of his sufferings by becoming like him (v.10). Now this is not to say that we become like Christ by imitating him. No, what Paul wanted to say that Christ made us his own (v.14). That is love language, reminding us of how in marriage love makes us belong to our lover and vice-versa. In faith we get married to Christ. And in a good marriage, you become a little like your beloved

49   John Chrysostom, "Homilies On Philippians," in *Nicene and Post-Nicene Fathers, First Series*, Vol.13, ed. Philip Schaff, p.238.

50   Ibid., p.235.

spouse. You share everything in common. Martin Luther once profoundly made that point. He wrote:

> *The third incomparable benefit of faith is that it unites the soul with Christ as a bride is united with her bridegroom. By this mystery, as the apostle teaches, Christ and the soul become one flesh. And if they are one flesh and there is between them a true marriage... it follows that everything they have they hold in common, the good as well as the bad.*[51]

Luther elaborated on this point. If we have all that Christ has, then you just spontaneously start doing Christ's thing. His thing was doing good, so Christians started doing good, just like without much thinking about it happily married couples start doing what pleases their lover:

> *It further follows from this that a Christian man living in this faith has no need of a teacher of good works... We may see this in an everyday example. When a husband and wife really love one another, have pleasure in each other, and thoroughly believe in their love, who teaches them how they are to behave one to another; what they are to do or not to do, say or not to say, what they are to think?*[52]

When you are engaged in a happy marriage, it changes you. After awhile you almost forget who you were before the relationship began! This is basically Paul's point, his prayer for us. The past is yesterday for one who has become like Jesus and been united with him. It just doesn't ultimately matter anymore.

---

51 Martin Luther, "The Freedom of a Christian" (1520), in *Luther's Works*, Vol. 31, p.351.

52 Martin Luther, "Treatise on Good Works" (1520), in *Luther's Works*, Vol. 44, pp.26-27.

It's like the American composer and poet John Cage once wrote: "We need not destroy the past. It is gone."

The past, all our efforts at justifying our goodness, pales in relation to Jesus. With the pressures of having to prove yourself and your status gone, off our backs, life gets a lot sweeter.

A book by social commentator Alain de Botton makes a profound point. He argues that much unhappiness in life is a function of anxiety about what others think of us — whether we matter, get attention, and are admired. By contrast, he notes, in religious devotion the differences between winners and losers fade, so that the concern about what others think of us (the cause of anxiety) fades.[53]

Martin Luther reflected on the text and noted its Good News. Celebrating the kind of alleviation from care that de Bottton notes he wrote: "Therefore a Christian, as a child of God, must always rejoice, always sing, fear nothing, always be free from care, and always glory in God."[54]

With the weight of the past gone, wrapped up in our relation with Jesus, there is nothing to fear, no more care. No wonder we sing songs in church. Feel the joy and freedom, for when we are wrapped up in Jesus and his future, nothing but joy is left, for everything else you've had in your life is overwhelmed by his love!

53   Alain de Botton, *Status Anxiety* (New York: Pantheon, 2004), esp. p.251.

54   Martin Luther, "Lectures on Hebrews" (1517-1518), in *Luther's Works*, Vol.29, p.177.

Passion Sunday
Philippians 2:5-11

God Doesn't Always Behave Like We Think He Should

In some ways life hasn't treated you like you wish it had, right? All the childhood dreams have not been fulfilled, have they? Some friends have been lost along the way. Beloved family members are gone. Maybe family life hasn't been quite what we'd hoped. The job's not all we thought it would be. You name it. For all of us life hasn't turned out just the way we had planned.

Life is not like the prosperity gospel preachers have promised.[55] God has not delivered on what they promised. He has not seemed to answer all our prayers. We have all had loved ones die.

In fact, we have a God who does things just the opposite from what we would expect God to do. This is what Martin Luther and his followers called the Theology of the Cross. Passion Sunday (Palm Sunday) especially illustrates this view of God. Along with our Bible lessons the theme of this Sunday gives a powerful witness, some solace, when we suffer or despair. We have a God who uses death to give life, who uses despair and disappointment to give hope (Deuteronomy 32:39).

---

55   Joel Osteen, *Your Best Life Now* (New York and Boston: Faith Words, 2004), pp.8,10.

The second lesson today provides a witness to these themes. Paul outlines how the eternal divine Son of God, though in the form of God, empties himself to take the form of a servant (v.7). And then Paul adds, citing a Christ hymn, no doubt sung in the early Church:

He humbled himself
and became obedient to the
    point of death —
even death on a cross (v.8).

Again it is evident that God works through vehicles that are apparently contrary to his aims. Through such lowly means, God achieves just the opposite, exalting Christ.

Paul adds in our lesson, still singing the same hymn:

so that at the Name of Jesus
every knee should bend,
in heaven and on earth and
under the earth,
and every tongue should confess
that Jesus Christ is Lord,
to the glory of God the Father. (vv.9-10).

The Palm Sunday/Holy Week sequence reflects God's inclination to confound us by doing just the opposite of what we would expect him to do. The king, the creator of the universe, comes to Jerusalem — on the foal of an ass (Luke 19:35ff). The glory of God sits on a humble ass. It is a study of contrasts. God works through contrasts and opposites.

There is more to the story and this pattern: The ordinary procession with Jesus on the colt was greeted in the big city as if it were the entourage of a king! The humble, ordinary-looking Jesus gets treated with the majesty that only a king deserves. God works through contrasts and opposites.

Then it happened again. The crowd who met Jesus that day praised and cheered him. They called him their king (Luke 19:36-38). Fickle people they were. Just five days later they deserted Jesus, while others called for his death (Luke 23:18ff.). Again it is evident that God works through contrasts and opposites.

The final act happens on the cross, as the crowd got its wish and saw Jesus put to death (Luke 23:33ff.). The one who is God was humbled and met death on a cross (vv. 6-8)! Yet, on that cross, Jesus not only found life for himself; forever his death became the passage to exaltation and life for others (vv. 9-11)! Think of it: Through the death of this ordinary-looking Hebrew peasant, forever and ever that death has been and will be the passageway to life! God has this thing about working through contrasts and opposites, about making good out of bad things, and about showing strength in the midst of apparent weakness. He just does not behave like most Americans think a god should. A 2008 poll by Baylor University found that more than half of us (52%) believe in a god who is either all-powerful and authoritative or distant.

What does this have to do with everyday life, with how we live? Passion Sunday and God's style of working good through contrasts and opposites, making good out of evil (the "Theology of the Cross," Martin Luther called it), explains the problems we talked about at the beginning of this sermon — how life has not turned out the way we wish, how the childhood dreams did not all come true, and how loved ones have been lost. God's style of working through contrasts and opposites helps explain why God often seems far away or irrelevant to everyday life.

Passion Sunday and Holy Week teach us that God works in hidden ways (like He used death on a cross to give life). God seems so powerless and distant sometimes, and then faith in him seems make no difference in our lives, wracked as they too often are with death, disappointment and pain. Our lesson and Palm Sunday remind us that this is God's style — to work in hidden ways and to make good out of evil.

Martin Luther nicely explained why and how God operates in these hidden, surprising ways. In a debate in 1518 he wrote:

> *He deserves to be called a theologian, however, who comprehends the visible and manifest things of God seen through suffering and the cross... Because men misused the knowledge of God through works, God wished again to be recognized in suffering and to condemn visible things so that those who did not honor God in his works should honor Him as He is hidden in his suffering.*[56]

Why does God operate in this way? He does it to exercise our faith. He makes us sinners. Again Luther's comments are clarifying:

> *Therefore since [God] can make just only those who are not just, he is compelled to perform an alien work in order to make them sinners before he performs his proper work of justification.*[57]

Here's the deal: By making himself seem absent from us, making it appear that he is powerless and unable to help, God brings out our sin and unbelief. Isn't that the way you are I are? It's easy to believe in

---

56 Martin Luther, "The Heidelberg Disputation" (1518), in *Luther's Works*, Vol. 31, p.52.

57 Martin Luther, "Sermon On St. Thomas' Day" (1516), in *Luther's Works*, Vol. 51, pp.19.

God when things are going good. But how about when things are rough on the job, when money is tight? How about when loved ones or friends are sick or passing? Then we are not so sure about God, about whether we really believe in him. No two ways about it: You and I are a lot like that fickle crowd waving the palms, who later called for Jesus' death. God working through opposites helps us see our sin more clearly.

Martin Luther put it this way:

> It is impossible for a person not to be puffed up by his good works unless he has first been deflated and destroyed by suffering and evil, until he knows that he is worthless and that his works are not his but God's.[58]

In a way, God doesn't always behave like we think he (a God) should in order to humble us. And if we're not humble, then we won't be ready for God's grace. We won't think we really need it enough. The first reformer said that expressly even before the Reformation. He wrote:

> A true Christian must have no glory of his own and must to such an extent be stripped of everything he calls his own... Therefore we must in all things keep ourselves so humble as if we still had nothing of our own. We must wait for the naked mercy of God, who will reckon us just and wise.[59]

You and I need humility to get ourselves out to the way, in order to appreciate the fact that we are totally dependent on God. He alone saves, and we need to get out of the way in order constantly to be reminded

---

58 Martin Luther, "The Heidelberg Disputation" (1518), in *Luther's Works*, Vol.31, p.53.

59 Martin Luther, "Lectures On Romans" (1515-1516), in *Luther's Works*, Vol.25, p.137.

that we're totally dependent on God. He alone saves us, and we bring nothing to the table when it comes to salvation.

It just makes sense: God hides himself and does not seem to answer our prayers, so that we experience unfaith and realize we are not so good that we "deserve" good treatment. We get our false gods and false sense of security destroyed in the midst of our doubts

Psychologist M. Scott Peck thinks it takes a self-emptiness to hear or care for another. He wrote: "We cannot let another person into our hearts and minds unless we empty ourselves. We can truly listen to him or truly hear her only out of emptiness." Mother Teresa, a believer who knew a good bit about giving this sort of love, explained it well. As she put it: "Love to be real, must cost, it must hurt, it must empty us of self."

The next time you feel these doubts or wonder about God, keep in mind that God doesn't behave like we think he should. Remember that we worship a God who works through contrasts and opposites. He did not send the doubts and hard times, but there ain't nothing so bad he can't make good out of it. He is making such doubts show us our lack of faith. Take heart: He's making good out of things. He is using those doubts to get us more ready to appreciate what he has done for us in saving us and using doubts to change us. We need a God who doesn't behave like we think he should in order to prod us to appreciate Easter, the grace of God, love and life a little more! Taking God for granted? Not seeing him in every aspect of your life? Start remembering that he doesn't behave like you think a God should, that he's more likely present in the midst of our doubts and questions. How good it is to have a God who goes against the grain!

In The Presence Of Christ!

... the Lord Jesus on the night when he was betrayed took a loaf of bread, and when he had given thanks, he broke it and said, "This is my body that is for you. Do this in remembrance of me." In the same way he took the cup also, after supper, saying, "This cup is the new covenant in my blood. Do this as often as you drink it, in remembrance of me." For as often as you eat this bread and drink the cup, you proclaim the Lord's death until he comes (vv.23-26).

The story of the institution of the Lord's Supper: What does it all mean for the church — for you? (What follows is an explanation of Christ's presence in the elements. Amendments should be made for others teaching that Christ is only spiritually present in the sacraments.)

For our church, when Christ says this *is* my body, we take it seriously. He is really in the bread and wine. But how can that be? And why does it matter? What benefit can the sacrament possibly have in our daily lives? And on top of that, how can we say that we receive the body and blood of our Lord, when what we really see and taste is mere bread and wine?

First, we are not teaching the Roman Catholic view of transubstantiation. It teaches that the consecrated bread and wine are no longer at the altar. The consecrated bread and wine might look like bread and wine, but they have been *changed*. That's why this view is called transubstantiation. The consecrated elements are now Jesus, no longer bread and wine.[60] No, our church still teaches that the elements remain bread and wine, but that Christ is *in* them. (Note: Other Protestants might amend this term accordingly, claiming instead that Christ is present among us in our celebration.)

How can Christ be present "in, with, and under" the bread and the wine?[61] What sense does this make? Are we engaged in meaningless double-talk here? And of what benefit is receiving this sacrament? What difference does it make in everyday life?

Let's be clear. The sacrament is a mystery. We cannot fully explain what happens and how. Yes, it's a mystery, but then we can get some handles on it.

First, what does all that talk of Christ being "in, with, and under" the bread and wine mean? If we take time to get clear on this, we'll find that there are any number of situations in life where two things are happening, and they are really one. One example that comes to mind is a burning coal (both coal and fire at once). How about a burning iron (fire and the iron) — two in one? We might also consider what happens in a hug between two lovers for each other. In one event we have both a physical embrace and love being really present.

We can make this point with a story: How about

---

60 *Catechism of the Catholic Church* (Collegeville, MN: This Liturgical Press, 1994), 1374-1375.

61 This phrase is found in the Lutheran *Formula of Concord*, Solid Declaration, in *The Book of Concord*, eds. Robert Kolb and Timothy J. Wengert, p.599.

a father who despite a very busy schedule takes time out from his work to bring his basketball-loving son to a game? Now anyone who was at that game nearby would see just that at the game — a man and his son. Yet for those who really knew the situation, they would see something else — would see the father's self-sacrificing love in action. But they would see that "in, with, and under" the act of a man taking his son to the game.

It is the same way with Christ's body and blood being simultaneously present in the bread and the wine. Like the people who knew the father and son could see love really present at the game, so we who know Christ, who have faith, can experience his presence whenever we celebrate this holy meal. And just like those at the game who did not know the father and his son, just see the two of them at the game, so without faith, the Lord's Supper looks just like eating bread and wine. (For those pastors of traditions just teaching that the bread and wine [or grape juice] are only symbols, preachers might explain the Sacrament in terms of the joy we experience with a pleasant memory, how love can be transmitted when we recall a loved one. And for those pastors of traditions which teach that the sacrament as a seal which when received brings us to Christ's heavenly presence, preachers might make the point how good it is to have a real encounter with a loved one, how much better actually to discourse with the loved one than merely to have a memory of it. And this is what happens when receiving the Lord's Supper in faith.)

All this is just information unless we know what good the Lord's Supper is for us. How is the receiving of Christ while eating and drinking relevant to everyday life? And how is it different from cannibalism? The answer is simple. It's all about Christ's presence, and that means it's all about love. Martin Luther explained this well in an Easter sermon:

But our dear Lord Christ desires that just as your greed speaks to you and preaches to you endlessly of money and good, or power and honor, in the same manner you would let yourself be drawn and led into that life, and think on your Redeemer, who died on the Cross for you; and so set your heart on fire, that you desire to be with him, being weary of this world...[62]

The Lord's Supper, receiving Christ, can set your heart on fire and make you desire him more. It's all about love. It is love and nothing but love that brought God to earth, to assume the form of a man, and finally to suffer and die for us. All this was done by God, because he loved us so much that he was willing to take upon himself the punishment we deserved. And in that broken, twisted body of Jesus of Nazareth, hanging on the cross, we see most clearly that self-sacrificing agape love. Likewise today, in the sacrament, as we receive again this broken body and spilled blood, we also see in the same clear manner what God has done on the cross. Like Luther says, being in his presence sets our hearts on fire to love him more.

Of course, this does not deny that God's love cannot be experienced outside the sacrament of Holy Communion. Indeed, God's love for us can be seen as well in the gifts of life, of family, of friends, and of material possessions, which he has given us. His love for us can also be seen in the gifts of schools and hospitals and in the church, which he has given us. Yet in all these things, while God's love is present, it's slightly hidden.

62   Martin Luther, "Easter Wednesday Sermon," in *The Complete Sermons of Martin Luther*, Vol. 6, ed. Eugene Klug, p.47.

Again an everyday example can be helpful. As men and women, each of us craves love from those closest to us and our loved ones have little different ways of showing love toward us. In the case of my wife Betsey, for instance (preachers might substitute examples with their own significant others), she often shows her love for me with a wink, cooking a favorite meal, or sometimes by telling me everything that happened to her during the day, even down to the smallest detail. All these are ways in which she tells me she loves me. But because she does not actually say the words that "she loves me" in these instances, they are somewhat veiled or hidden expressions of love. But when she takes me in her arms and tells me of her love, then I know for sure.

To continue the analogy, on the cross and in the sacraments, God is taking each one of us individually into his arms and telling us he loves us — in such a way that there's no mistaking it. This is the whole meaning of receiving Jesus in the bread and the wine. We are actually having physical contact with him when we receive the Communion elements. It is like a hug or kiss from Jesus. (Preachers of other traditions might refer to an intimate conversation with or fond recollection of him.)

Sometimes when life goes bad, when there is illness death, God's other ways of telling us he loves us are not very clear. But never when it comes to the sacrament. For here at the foot of the cross there is no mistaking it. For in the body and blood of his Son, God shouts his love for us loudly and clearly enough — that the whole universe can hear.

As you come now before the altar, you need not come with fear or unnecessary seriousness. Come with joy and happiness. For waiting here is the presence of Christ, a loving God, ready to clasp you in his arms and tell you of his love.

Good Friday
Hebrews 10:16-25

Look What Happened On The Cross!
Christ Burns Away All Our Pettiness

Americans (human beings) are very divided. Some of our divisions have to do with who we are. Black-white tensions caused by the police killings of Black men have made the divisions clearer. A 2016 Pew Research poll found that while 61% of African-Americans find Black-white relations poor, only 46% of whites have such an assessment. The election of Donald Trump verified the polls' findings regarding negative American attitudes toward immigrants. We are badly divided by social class, regardless of ethnicity, as eminent social commentator Charles Murray has pointed out. He has found few commonalities professional and working class people share (how little people from different classes know each other's likes and dislikes).[63] We are also divided by religion. Good Friday is a time to confess our sins, because our divisions brought Christ to the cross.

Do you agree? Are we as a nation not divided? Think of the tensions in your personal or professional life. Confess them. Think of the people you don't enjoy much. Good Friday is a time to confess your sins. Your sins and mine are the reason Jesus went to the cross.

63 Charles Murray, *Coming Apart: The State of White America, 1960-2010* (New York: Cox and Murray, 2012).

Divisions like we have been considering are consequences of how you look at life. When we are in conflict, it is a function of our making judgments about our neighbors and finding them wanting. It happens when we evaluate our reality and those around us in accord with certain rules of behavior and being. When you do that you are living under the law, operating with certain demands that people need to live up to, and then you judge them. This is living under the old covenant (Exodus 19:5). But our lesson declares that Christ's sacrificial work has replaced that way of doing business with the new covenant. Today, on the cross, Christ the high priest has ushered in the new covenant (v.15). That's what Good Friday is all about.

This new covenant is characterized by forgiveness, not by the judgmentalism of the old covenant which has led to all our tensions (vv.17-18). When you have Christ, you are already holy and righteous, John Calvin says. Christ is the fountain of both.[64]

Our lesson elaborates further on this point. The new covenant, it says, gives us confidence to enter the temple sanctuary, and so in that sense, direct access to God (vv.19-20). And this gives us full assurance of being free from an evil conscience (vv.22-23)! Methodist founder John Wesley nicely makes this point:

> As by rending the veil in the temple, the holy of holies became visible and accessible, so by wounding the body of Christ, the God of heaven was manifested and the way to heaven opened.[65]

64 John Calvin, "Commentaries On the Epistle of St. Paul To the Hebrews" (1549), in *Calvin's Commentaries*, Vol. XXII/1, trans. James Anderson, p.236.

65 John Wesley, *Commentary On the Bible*, ed. G. Roger Schoenhals (Grand Rapids, MI: Francis Asbury Press, 1990), p.568.

Freed from judgment in this way, you and I are also set free from judging others!

Hear that? Good Friday is about the end of being judgmental. On the cross, God has made it clear that he is not in judgment about us. And when you are not judged yourself, you won't find yourself needing to judge others so much anymore. When judgments of others stop, you won't find yourself so divided from others either.

In line with this thinking, the author of Hebrews (it was probably not Paul, but someone belonging to the generation of his young followers), proceeds to note that in view of this new way Christ's sacrifice has created, we are to look for ways to provoke each other to good deeds, meeting together, and encouraging each other (vv.24-25). Christ's sacrificial work on the cross brings us together and, like I noted, overcomes the divisions we've been considering.

What happened on the cross is that Jesus died for *all* of us! The divisions are gone (unless we introduce them again). Political arguments and racial and gender differences did not matter to Jesus on the cross. What then should matter to us?

Martin Luther says that "he who relies on Christ through faith is carried on the shoulders of Christ..."[66] We are all on those shoulders together, and so no need to be divided. There's no room for squabbling on Christ's shoulders. The ancient Greek poet Aesop said it well: "In union there is strength." Likewise, the nineteenth-century American poet George Pope Morris well summarized the point of this lesson: "United we stand, divided we fall."

66   Martin Luther, "Lectures on Hebrews" (1517-1518), in *Luther's Works*, Vol. 29, p.226.

The great preacher of the early church John Chrysostom was commenting on verse 24 of our lesson and its reference to provoking one another to love and good deeds. He proclaimed:

For if a stone rubbed against a stone sends forth fire, how much more soul mingled with soul.[67]

We are set on fire with love for each other. But how does the fire start? Of course it begins with Jesus and what he did that day on the cross. The fire in our hearts is lit by God. Founder of the Quakers William Penn said it well, that coals from God must kindle our fire. You need God in Christ to set your heart on fire, the fire of love that can make you overcome divisions.

When you are on fire with this kind of love, all the divisions get burned away. John Wesley's brother Charles made a penetrating observation: "Catch on fire with enthusiasm and people will come for miles to watch you burn," he said. The fire of God's love attracts people.

No two ways about it. Life is so much better, so much more in harmony, we are so much more unified, because Jesus put us all on his shoulders and died this day for each and every single human being. No room for squabbling on Jesus' shoulders no matter how broad those shoulders are. That's what makes this Friday *good*. His sacrifice burns away all the divisions among us, burns down all the pettiness of the present order of things, and sets you and me and all the faithful on fire with his love! His fire turns us into subversive rebels towards the ways of the world.

---

67   John Chrysostom, "Homilies On Epistle To Hebrews," in *Nicene and Post-Nicene Fathers*, First Series, Vol.14, ed. Philip Schaff, p.455.

Good Friday
Hebrews 4:14-16; 5:7-9

A Sympathetic High Priest

Whoever wrote this sermon (it is not likely that it was Paul, since its style is different from other books written by Paul) was addressing a group of Jewish Christians. But what he has to say is for us, especially at this time when we remember Christ's death:

Since then we have a great high priest who passed through the heavens, Jesus, the Son of God, let us hold fast to our confession. For we do not have a high priest who is unable to sympathize with our weaknesses, but we have one who in every respect has been tested... (4:14-15)

Yes, we have a great high priest who passed through the heavens. Jesus, the high priest who performed the greatest of all sacrifices, offered himself on the cross to die for us. We all knew that. This is what Good Friday is all about.

And we also knew that Jesus' high priestly work was vindicated on Easter, that he passed through the clouds in victory when he ascended into heaven. But the idea that he sympathizes with our weaknesses, that he was tested, that doesn't go down quite as easily for us. It's not very American. We've previously noted that, according to a 2008 poll by Baylor University, more than half of us (52%) believe in a god who is either all-powerful and authoritative or distant. A god like that would not be tested. Our lesson which says that Jesus was tested is about Jesus' humanity, not his status as Son of God! Really?

What does it mean to say that Jesus is two natures, but one person? The famous ancient African theologian Origen provides a helpful image. He suggests we think of Jesus' divinity and humanity as fire and iron (two substances) which become one burning iron.[68]

Think about this image. If you have a burning iron, what happens to the fire happens to the iron. Throw water on one, the other gets doused. Try to touch one, you touch them both.

Well the man Jesus suffered. That means the Son of God suffered too. God suffered too!

But that goes against the grain of the all-powerful god in whom Americans believe. That is exactly the point.

Famed Christian Martyr Dietrich Bonhoeffer, a man who was killed for trying to stop Hitler's atrocities, firmly believed in a suffering god. It was a teaching that distinguishes Christianity from other religions he claimed:

> Here is the decisive difference between Christianity and all religions. Man's religiosity makes him look in distress to the power of God in the world. God is the deus ex machina [the God of the machine who intervenes in the action].

68   "Origen, On First Principles," in *Ante-Nicene Fathers*, Vol.4, eds. Alexander Roberts and James Donaldson, p.283. This is a view of Lutheranism; see *Formula of Concord*, Solid Declaration (1577), in *The Book of Concord*, eds. Robert Kolb and Timothy J. Wengert, p.619. This image is typical of ancient Alexandrian Christology. Preachers from traditions with an Antiochene Christology, not believing that what happens to Christ's humanity does not impact his divinity, may want to focus the sermon on how Jesus' human nature can empathize with our suffering.

The Bible directs man to God's powerlessness and suffering; only the suffering God can help... [This] opens up a way of seeing the God of the Bible, Who wins power and space in the world by His weakness.[69]

How are God's suffering and weakness helpful for God to gain power in the world? What good is a weak God?

The framer of Black Liberation Theology James Cone, who also teaches that God suffers, helps us understand these issues. He wrote:

In Christ God enters human affairs and takes sides with the oppressed. Their suffering becomes his; their despair, divine despair. Through Christ the poor are offered freedom now to rebel against that which makes them other than human.[70]

A suffering God is one who identifies with our suffering. He suffers with those who are suffering, does not just express empathy or regret. Cone says that this makes the suffering and despair that the poor and oppressed endure *divine!* The suffering and the despair have meaning. The ancient theologian Archelaus said that the suffering god endures in Christ relieves us of having to "to suffer any pain to no purpose."[71] If it's divine suffering you and I experience, it must have a purpose.

69   Dietrich Bonhoeffer, *Letters and Papers from Prison,* ed. Eberhard Bethge (New York: Macmillan, 1968),p.188.

70   James Cone, *Risks of Faith: The Emergence of a Black Theology of Liberation,* 1968-1998 (Boston: Beacon, 1999), p.8.

71   Archelaus, *The Disputation With Manes, in Ante-Nicene Fathers, Vol.6,* eds. Alexander Roberts and James Donaldson (2nd print.; Peabody, MA: Hendrickson, 1995), p.217.

This is the space, this is the power God creates for Himself by suffering in Jesus Christ. This suffering God's place is not in heaven, but is right beside you and me in the hurts of life. And that is a powerful place. Think how life works. The people in your life whom you can most lean on are ones who have been there with us or have experienced something like we have. The grieving feel they can best relate to someone else who has lost a loved one. Somebody who's lost as job gets more comfort and understanding from someone who lost a job too, especially if it's with the same employer. The addict relates best to another addict, the war vet with a war vet.

Now that is who God is. In Jesus Christ, he has related Himself to us in our trials and struggles with sin. God has experienced your and my weaknesses, he knows what it's like to suffer, he knows what it's like to feel worthless and abandoned, he knows what it's like to face death. Remember when Bill Clinton was president, and with his southern accent he would tell us he could "feel our pain." Well, God is not like Bill Clinton, from a distance feeling your pain. No, God is like the loving parent who hurts when her child is crying, the widow comforting another widow, the close friend or war buddy who's been there with you in the fears and suffering, all of them reflecting what God is always doing for you and me. And that is power. The people in your life who have been there with you have extraordinary influence and impact on your life, right? That's what Dietrich Bonhoeffer meant when he said that God wins power by his weakness.

And yet it is not power that God in Christ wants on the cross. Just like those who suffer with us become vulnerable with us, don't act like they have all the answers since they are struggling with us, that's the way God operates according to Martin Luther. God comes to console us. Luther once wrote:

> *Therefore the apostle also introduces Christ here more as a priest than as a lord and judge, in order that he may console those who are frightened.*[72]

An appreciation that you have someone in your life (God in Christ) who has and will again go to the mat for you overcomes a lot of fear, gets you ready to face life. That is why our lesson says that we can now approach the throne of grace, relate to God, with boldness (4:16). This alleviation of fear also results in happiness. Again Luther puts it well:

> *Therefore a Christian, as a child of God, must always rejoice, always sing, fear nothing, always be free from care, and always glory in God.*[73]

How does a God who suffers with us make a difference? What is the outcome for daily life of this joy? This joy leads to gratitude and a hope that conquers all the uncertainty, the suffering, the sadness we are enduring in life. Again Martin Luther helps us see the matter more clearly:

> *We do not preach about the passion in order for people to become ingrates; but rather that they recognize our heavenly Father's great love for humankind and his son our Lord Jesus Christ... For he who believes with his whole heart that Christ suffered for him will not be a thankless rogue, but will with his whole being be grateful to*

---

72 Martin Luther, "Lectures on Hebrews" (1517-1518), in *Luther's Works,* Vol.29, p.167.

73 Ibid., p.177.

Christ. If someone came to my rescue in an emergency, when death threatened by fire or water, I would have to be a wretch not to feel grateful toward him.[74]

Filled with this kind of gratitude, no matter how bad things look, Christians see Jesus on the cross and gratefully see God suffer for them, both on Easter and in the tragedies of their own lives. But we Christians also know that Easter is coming. We have hope buoyed by our sympathetic God that things will be all right in the long run. Dietrich Bonhoeffer beautifully reminds us of this realistic hope. As he put it:

Where there is still hope, there is no defeat; there may be every kind of weakness, much clamor and complaining, much anxious shouting; nevertheless, because hope is present, the victory has already been won.[75]

The cross, an awareness that God is in the trenches with you, suffering with you — does not guarantee a life without hassles — a life without tragedy. (Bonhoeffer after all met death.) But with the knowledge that God in Christ is right there with you, you have the hope you need to struggle against the injustice, and that hope and gratitude is all you need (as it is said in the black church) "to keep on keep'in on." And when that happens, Bonhoeffer and Easter remind us on this Friday that it is really Good — the victory is already won!

---

74   Martin Luther, "Good Friday House Postil Sermon" (1533), in *The Complete Sermons of Martin Luther,* Vol.5, ed. Eugene Klug, pp.473-474.

75   Dietrich Bonhoeffer, "The Secret of Suffering' (1538), in *A Testament To Freedom,* eds. Geffrey B. Kelly and F. Burton Nelson (New York: Harper San Francisco, 1990), p.307

Why The Resurrection Makes Sense

*If for this life only we have hoped in Christ, we are of all peo-
ple most to be pitied. But in fact Christ has been raised from
the dead, the first fruits of those who have died. (vv.19-20)*

Christ is risen! But is it true? Where's the proof? The
world and life-experience say there is no proof. In fact,
if the great existentialist philosopher of the twentieth
century Albert Camus is right, there is nothing in our
world that isn't arbitrary. Camus contends ultimately
all there is to life is chaotic meaninglessness. There are
no values unless we assert them for ourselves. But ultimately it does not matter. All there is in life is the con-
stant flow of meaningless existence, filled with misery
and evil, ultimately culminating in death. What's the
use?[76]

The resurrection matters to Christians, but does
it make sense to the world? It matters to Christians,
because had Jesus not risen, it is likely that his cult
would have faded into oblivion with his death. It is
only because of reports of his resurrection that Jesus'
small group of followers kept his word alive. There is
a famous modern German theologian Wolfhart Pan-
nenberg who makes the point in a most penetrating
way: "The answer to the question 'Did Jesus really rise

[76]   Albert Camus, *The Rebel*, trans. Anthony Bower (New York: Vintage,
1956), esp. p.101.

from the dead?' is absolutely decisive for any Christian proclamation and for Christian faith itself."

Yet for all its importance and weight in Christian faith through the ages, the resurrection of Jesus has come to be viewed as an embarrassment, not unlike how the belief was under fire in Paul's day. That's why in our lesson he perceived the need to assert the resurrection in face of skeptics (v.20). Have you struggled with the belief that a dead body could come back to life?

The world, in all its chaos about meaning and values, finds it hard to accept. And methods used by professional historians entail that a resurrection is not possible (because when reports from the past have no analogy in present experience their veracity needs to be challenged).[77] No wonder, then, if some of us have a tough time believing the bodily resurrection. A lot of modern historians do. A 2016 Rasmussen Report poll found that nearly 1 in 4 of us (23%) don't believe Jesus is risen. Paul says we all need to believe it. Let's see if he and I can close the deal on this, since the resurrection is so central to our faith.

Now first, let's be clear that if you are having problems believing the historical truth of other miracles in the Bible, then the other miracle accounts or even the creation story don't have the same weight as Jesus' resurrection. In fact, in principle, you can still be a member in good standing in this church if you have trouble with the Jonah account or that the flood was God's will in part in punishment for the birth of divine-human Nephilim to human mothers (see Genesis 6:4). But not

---

77   The suppositions of the historian are described by Ernst Troeltsch, *Gesammelte Schriften*, *Vol.2* (Tübingen: J.C.B. Mohr, 1913), pp.729-753; see my *The Integrity of Biblical Narrative: Story In Theology and Proclamation* (Minneapolis: Fortress Press, 1990), esp. p.14.

so regarding the resurrection. If you can't accept that — you will not be able to go along with everything else that Christian faith says about Jesus.

The Bible makes this point elsewhere in a way, in John (11:25). Jesus calls himself there the resurrection and the life. In Romans (1:4) Paul says that Jesus has been designated Son of God by the resurrection! Get the point? You do not know the Jesus portrayed by the New Testament if he is someone who has not risen! The logic of Christian faith entails that if you accept the authority of the Bible, if that is where you know Jesus and accept its version of him, then it makes no sense to deny that Jesus is risen.

Now this is not a blind faith. In fact, we can make the case for it like a lot of other scientific claims. Let me break this down for you. True enough, we have not observed Jesus' resurrection ourselves. But it is a pre-supposition (could we call it a paradigm) that is crucial for making sense of Christian faith. As Christians we could say that this is a crucial assumption/paradigm for understanding the world.

Know any other paradigms like this? Ever see gravity? We've seen the results, but not a thing called gravity. And yet because it well explains things, we endorse the supposition. How about atoms? Same. No one has seen an atom, but we widely accept the theory because it is a paradigm that helps us understand other data that we can observe. It is the same with the theory of evolution or the strings of string theory.

These are scientific claims, and yet they have not been proven. What makes them scientific claims? We need to consider how the scientific method works.[78]

78   For this outline of the Scientific Method I am indebted to Tomas Kuhn, *The Structure of Scientific Revolutions* (2nd ed; Chicago: University of Chicago Press, 1970).

Experiments cannot prove everything that we consider to be scientifically accurate. Rather, scientific discoveries proceed with the formulation of new paradigms which are developed to make sense of observed data. If we don't do that, we come away like the existentialist philosopher Albert Camus with the conclusion that life is chaotically meaningless. As more and more members of the scientific community find a given theory/paradigm helpful, it becomes recognized as an accepted theory and informs more research. But if data disproves a theory, it is rejected and science moves on in search of improved, more verifiable new paradigms. This explains how human beings have moved from an earth-centered universe to a helio-centered universe, from the belief that nature was like a machine to today's present appreciation that the universe is more like an organism.

Let's look, then, at Jesus' resurrection on the first Easter, see it in these categories as a paradigm for looking at the world.[79] The paradigm certainly emerges from the data with which we have to work — the Bible and the Christian tradition which demand acknowledgment that Jesus' resurrection is essential to how you understand Christianity. And there is a lot of evidence that this paradigm (the belief that death is overcome by life) helps us better understand the world and live in it. Think of the two millennia that people calling themselves Christians have advanced civilization and helped Christians to cope with a sense of life's meaninglessness that the existentialist philosopher we met

---

79   A lot what follows is found in my book *The Integrity of Biblical Narrative: Story In Theology and Proclamation*, pp.36-51, and I am indebted to Hans Frei, *The Identity of Jesus Christ* (Philadelphia: Fortress, 1975), p.151.

at the beginning of this sermon described. These kinds of arguments are right in line with scientific methods of verification.

Scientific theories can be disproved. Well, it's the same with Jesus' resurrection. No, we don't have to prove he rose in the hard sense of proof, just like no hard proof has been given to support the existence of atoms or evolution. But just as data could in principle disprove these theories, so if the bones of Jesus were found (they have not been), or if it were demonstrated that Christianity does not help its adherents cope, then the conclusion would be that the resurrection is not true and so Christianity in not true![80]

Get the point, Christian? The truth claimed for the resurrection has parallels to the claims of scientific truth! The resurrection may not be provable in the hard sense, like a mathematical equation. But it certainly makes sense. It has as much credibility as atomic theory, evolution, and the goodness of democracy. So let's stop being so uncertain or uneasy in our faith. *Jesus is risen!* Happy Easter. The resurrection makes sense.

So what? What difference does it make? Paul gives us an answer in our lesson. Death has been destroyed, he claims (v.26). Later in the chapter from which our lesson is taken, he claims that all things have been subjected to the Son so that God may be all in all (v.28). What a treasure Easter is. We need no longer fear death or anything else. Martin Luther nicely pointed out in one of his 1,532 sermons that the world has nothing to offer compared to the marvels of the resurrection:

80 Others contending that historical or sociological evidence would count against Christian claims include George Lindbeck, *The Nature of Doctrine* (Philadelphia: Westminster, 1984), pp.131,68; Julian Hartt, "Reply to Crites and Hauerwas," *Journal of the American Academy of Religion 52, No. 1* (March 1984): 156,155.

Behold, thus we must view our treasure and turn away from temporal reality that lies before our eyes and sense. We must not let death and other misfortune, distress and misery, terrify us so. Nor must we regard what the world has and can do, but balance this against what we are and have in Christ. For our confidence is built entirely on the fact that he has risen and that we have life with him already and are no longer in the power of death. Therefore let the world be made and foolish, boasting and relying on its money and goods.[81]

Now it's true that you and I do not always have this confidence, still sometimes struggle with the resurrection. No, we are still caught up in sin, too concerned with our own lives and not enough concerned with others, still wondering if life really has meaning, still too fretful about dying. But Easter promises serenity, a new life of which Christ is the first fruit, a life not craving the things of the world so much.

Again Martin Luther describes the risen Lord and what Easter is all about in compelling ways. He proclaimed:

Therefore if you believe in Christ, you must not flee from him or be frightened; for here you perceive and see that his whole heart, mind, or thinking are intent only on rescuing you from all that assails and oppresses you and on placing you with Christ over everything.[82]

Easter testifies to the fact that we have a God who is wholly devoted to rescuing us from all that assails us and made us people who care nothing for the world

---

81 Martin Luther, "Commentary On 1 Corinthians 15 (1532)," in *Luther's Works*, Vol.28, p.111.

82 Ibid., pp.139-140.

except Jesus. When we get caught up in that way then all the doubts about the resurrection would whither. Catch the Easter vision that Jesus has his whole heart and mind and thinking devoted to you, that all he wants is to rescue you, then, the importance of the things of this world, doubts occasioned by the apparent meaninglessness of life begin to fade and the common sense of Jesus' Easter Resurrection begins to make even more sense. And like other scientific findings — this one makes a lot more sense of life for you.

Easter Makes Us One!

What Martin Luther King Jr. wrote in 1963 is still true today. He stated, "We have learned to fly the air like birds and swim the sea like fish, but have not learned the simple art of living together as brothers [and sisters]." Dr. King is still correct. The Trump election made clear our attitudes towards Muslim immigrants. A *Detroit News* poll conducted over a decade ago (in 2007) is still relevant. It found that nearly half of the local white population preferred to live in an all-white neighborhood. The Census Bureau found that the median household income for American families was $55,775 in 2015, but only $36,544 for African-American households.

Racial attitudes are very much alive. General Social Survey found in 2016 that 55% of white Republicans believed that African-Americans were more likely to be impoverished because of a lack of motivation and willpower. We've previously noted how divided we are by social class, as professionals and the working classes do not live near each other, do not exhibit the same values or levels of religiosity, do not have the some pop-culture icons, and do not even follow the same sports.[83] We are clearly far removed from Dr. King's call for living in community.

83   For specifics, see Charles Murray, *Coming Apart: The State of White America, 1960-2010*.

Peter gave a sermon one time that speaks to these concerns. Here's the background on the sermon that's reported in the second lesson we are using. He had been summoned to Caesarea, a port on the Mediterranean Sea about fifty miles to the northwest of Jerusalem, by Cornelius, a devout Gentile who was also a commanding officer in the Roman army (vv.5-8,17-23). Meanwhile, Peter had had a vision teaching him that the Gentiles were not unclean (vv.10-16).

This miraculous series of events had led the apostle to give up his Jewish practices of maintaining social distance from Gentiles lest such fraternization render him impure and displease God (v.28). He began socializing with his Gentile host Cornelius and his emissaries (vv.23,27-29). We pick up this story with the sermon he delivered explaining why this behavior transpired.

What does all this have to do with Easter? We are getting to the point. Peter does it for us. In his sermon explaining God's will to overcome barriers, he invokes the Resurrection (vv.35ff.). Get it? For Peter, Easter is all about overcoming barriers. Jesus rose for all!

Peter makes this point to some extent when he says *everyone* who believes in Christ receives forgiveness of sins (v.43) — *everyone*. Easter breaks down the barriers. Christ rose for all.

John Wesley made this point very nicely. He wrote:

[God] Is not partial in his love... He is loving to every man and wills that all men should be saved.[84]

The Word of God is not partial in his love. This entails that Easter is for everybody!

We need this word to help break down barriers in America, to become a nation that is committed to

84 John Wesley, *Commentary On the Bible*, ed. G. Roger Schoenhals, p.480.

our unity. Martin Luther King Jr powerfully explained how Christ's work brings people together and the social ethical implications of this. In a 1967 sermon he proclaimed:

> *But in Christ there is neither Jew nor Gentile. In Christ there is neither male nor female. In Christ there is neither Communist or capitalist. In Christ, somehow there is neither bound or free. We are all one in Christ Jesus. And when we truly believe in the sacredness of human personality, we won't exploit people, we won't trample over people with iron feet of oppression, we won't kill anybody.*[85]

A nation that continues trampling people, oppressing them, and failing to celebrate our unity contradicts the good news of the empty tomb.

Now some may say we live in a post-racial society, that we are a nation which elected a Black president. But that overlooks the anti-immigrant attitudes, and the Black-white economic disparities noted at the beginning of this sermon. Don't forget that even though we may get along with folks of different ethnicities on the job or at meetings, we don't typically socialize or even live near each other. The census bureau has provided statistics demonstrating that despite minority growth and increased minority dispersion to the suburbs, the average white resident lives in a neighborhood that has become only modestly more diverse and remains markedly "whiter" than its respective metropolitan area population.

In small towns, the average American in these locales lives in communities that are 80% white. Mean-

---

85   Martin Luther King, Jr., "A Christmas Sermon on Peace" (1967), in *A Testament of Hope*, ed. James M. Washington, P.255.

while Sunday worship remains the most segregated hour in this "Christian" nation of ours. We keep bashing the immigrants who don't speak English and "those welfare chiselers" who more than likely are of a different ethnicity than our own.

No, America needs the kind of inclusivity that Paul and Martin Luther King, Jr call us to note. This inclusivity, rooted in God's love is good for us. Good for America. Recall Dr. King's comments about how we are all one in Christ, that in faith we "won't exploit people, we won't trample them."[86] Yes, we are better for being inclusive. Literacy coordinator Joe Bishop says it well: "If we're going to live up to our potential, then we need to be inclusive of everybody." In fact, we're more fully human when we are cooperating together. Scholars of evolution have observed that what gives homo sapiens the edge on Earth has been our superior ability to cooperate.[87] An inclusive nation, prodded by the church's Easter word of inclusivity, will be a happier, nicer, more fully human place.

In view of the benefits that being inclusive like Jesus and Peter were, it is obvious that Martin Luther had it right. He said that this lesson was a "comforting message, a gospel of joy and grace, a message not accusing, threatening and terrifying..."[88] What a comforting message to know that everyone can have forgiveness of sin. No one has priority (or more properly, everyone is God's priority).

86   Ibid.

87   See Nicholas Wade, *The Faith Instinct* (New York: Penguin, 2009), esp. pp.54ff.

88   Martin Luther, "Sermon On Easter Monday," in *The Complete Sermons of Martin Luther, Vol.4/1*, ed. John Lenker (Grand Rapids, MI: Baker Books, 2000), p.195.

The American Catholic Bishops in a 1979 statement said it so beautifully. After condemning racism the bishops claimed that "Christ's face is the composite of all persons."[89] In Jesus, in what he did and is, we can see all of us — all the different races, ethnicities, and social classes.

Easter proclaims that everyone is a forgiven sinner. And forgiven sinners like us, no longer burdened by fear of punishment on account of sin, can be brave. We can be brave because we know that we are acceptable in God's sight, and that Jesus has overcome all the roadblocks. We can also be brave because we are all in this together, all heirs of the resurrection. And in this unity, there is strength.

Of course we'll be celebrating this, celebrating Easter, next Sunday too. We do it each Sunday, because, as you may know, the reason for worshiping Sunday and not on the Jewish sabbath, Saturday, was to celebrate the Easter resurrection in every worship service. That's why Easter, the celebration of our unity, is not over today. The unity created by Easter is a year-round thing for us. To celebrate Easter all year is to celebrate it and work with others in unity.

---

89   U.S. Catholic Bishops, "Brothers and Sisters to Us" (1979).

Easter 2
Revelation 1:4-8

The Power Of The Resurrection

Christ is risen! Risen indeed!

I should have warned you last week when I was praising what a marvelous thing Jesus' resurrection is that we might not feel the joy and reality of Christ's resurrection this week like we did last Sunday. It's true, isn't it? Last Sunday's high didn't last the whole week, did it? And as for today, the church's isn't packed like last week. That sense of enthusiasm isn't as apparent. We're not as certain in our faith. Why not?

Maybe Christ hasn't risen after all. After all, things seem pretty much the same. Nothing new. This Sunday is supposed to be devoted to considering the fruits of the resurrection. For historically, the second Sunday of Easter was a day during which newly baptized members would be admitted into the fellowship as full members.[90]

Where are the fruits? Where are the fruits in our lives? Why don't we feel them? Why don't we feel the fruits of the resurrection on a daily basis in our lives? Is it possible that Jesus really has not risen?

In trying to sort out this set of problems, in trying to come to terms without doubts or at least our lack of enthusiasm about our faith, the book of Revelation is a good place to start. Revelation was written to Christians who felt some anxiety about their faith. We may

90   Luther Reed, *The Lutheran Liturgy*, p.509.

not be being persecuted like these early Christians were, but we are experiencing some of the same feelings that these first Christians did concerning God's absence. And so the book of Revelation's word of hope to them is as word of hope to us.

Martin Luther said the same thing so well in 1530 when he wrote a kind of introduction to the book of Revelation. He wrote:

Some of the know-it-alls are even doing that very thing. They see heresy and dissension and shortcomings of many kinds; they see that there are many false, many loose-living Christians...

They ought to read this book [Revelation] and learn to look upon Christendom with other eyes than those of [their] reason... A Christian is even hidden from himself;he does not see his holiness and virtue, but sees in himself nothing but unholiness and vice...

In a word, our holiness is in heaven where Christ is, and not in the world before men's eyes... If only the word of the gospel remains pure among us, and we love and cherish it, we shall not doubt that Christ is with us, even when things are at their worst. As we shall see in this book [in Revelation], that through and beyond all... evil... Christ is nonetheless with his saints, and wins the final victory.[91]

Let me run those works of Luther by you again: Let evil, sloth, lack of enthusiasm, and doubts do what they can. Christ has won the final victory! Christ has conquered them all.

I spent so long on this quote, telling you what Luther said about the book of Revelation, because it's a

91   Martin Luther, "Prefaces To the New Testament" (1546/1522), in *Luther's Works*, Vol.35, pp.410-411.

wonderful exposition of our second lesson today. Besides, Luther has spoken to us here about the problems we may be having concerning a lack of confidence or a lack of excitement that we may feel in our faith.

Luther spoke of the fact that our holiness is in heaven where Christ is. He added that Christ has won the victory over all our doubts, over all the sin and evil in the world, over all the things that undermine Christianity's credibility in the world, like our own and the Church's hypocrisy. Christ has triumphed over all that.

Our second lesson makes this point. And then after the lesson ends, the author of Revelation reports a preparatory vision he had (vv.9-20). And in that vision, on the Lord's day, he is whisked in his dream into heaven. And he sees "one like a Son of Man, clothed with a long robe... his head and his hair white and snow, with eyes like a flame of fire... (vv.13-14) This is the risen and exalted Christ!

That it is Christ we encounter becomes even clearer in the dream. This one like the Son of Man is so overwhelming that the writer of Revelation reportedly faints away, as though dead. But the Lord teaches him, comforts him, and says (echoing the last verse of our lesson): *Do not be afraid; I am the First and the Last, and the Living One; I was dead and see, I am alive forever and ever...* (vv.17-18) No doubt about it. It was the exalted heavenly Christ that we and the writer of Revelation encounter.

Next Christ uttered the punch line: ... *I have the keys of death and of hades.* (v.19) Christ has died and now will live forever. We see that in our lesson where the Lord God is said to be the one *who is and who was and who is to come...* (v.8) Christ lives forever, for he has conquered death and hell. This is the message of our second lesson. It says that he has freed us by his blood (v.5). That's what Martin Luther says, we've noticed.

This is the antidote that Revelation and Luther's version of it offer for our doubts, our apathy, our lack of enthusiasm and commitment to our faith. The formula is a very simple one here: You need encounters with the risen Lord; you need to experience the risen and victorious Christ in order to be assured of his resurrection and in order to be nurtured in a living faith. When we have Christ and his conquest in our hearts, then we can truly persevere and revel in faith — then Christianity truly comes alive for us. Christ is victorious. And he is present with us here. He is present in our fellowship. He is present in the word proclaimed, present in the liturgy, and most clearly present in the bread and wine we eat in the Lord's Supper. Behold the risen Christ, the victor over sin and death, in our presence.

Of course if all that's true, then we've got a problem, don't we? The problem is that we, Luther, and the writer of our second lesson all proclaim that Christ has conquered, that he is victorious, that he holds the keys of death and hell. Really? Has Christ really conquered? If so, what has He conquered? Why is there still so much apathy, hypocrisy, and doubt in the church? Why are so many turned off by Christianity or live in regions where the gospel has never been preached? Why is there so much evil, violence, poverty, and oppression in our world? How can anybody in their right mind say that Christ has conquered — that he holds the keys to death and hell? Now that is a problem. It is the problem of Christianity's credibility, is it not? What do you think?

I will tell you how I have sorted this one out for myself. The book of Revelation has helped me think it through. In Revelation you have these scenes, like in today's second lesson or in chapter 12, where the risen Christ is proclaimed or shown to be victorious over sin and evil. But then in the same book you have many examples like in chapter 20, in chapters 13 and 9, and also in verse 9 of the chapter we consider today where it seems that sin and evil still have their way in the world. Somehow John (the man to whom tradition ascribes the authorship of Revelation) and our Lord felt that the people to whom Revelation was addressed would be comforted in their suffering and doubts by glimpses of Christ's heavenly glory and by reminders that He has vanquished evil and death. Our faith and enthusiasm for our faith can be invigorated by such glimpses and assurances that in Christ, we Christians are on the winning team. And that seems to be the point of the book of Revelation — to proclaim that Christ has conquered. He sits in heaven enthroned. But the war is not over yet on earth. The war isn't over yet.

This image of a victor, even though the war isn't yet over, opens an avenue for understanding the book of Revelation and the reality of our faith. Sometimes in a war, the victory is assured, because one side has won the major and decisive battle. But then there's still mop-up operations or follow-up battles to be fought. We might consider the American Civil War. It is like the North's position after that Battle of Gettysburg. The South had been defeated at Gettysburg, the North had effectively won the war by stopping Southern incursions in the North, but there were a lot of battles still to be fought.

Think of the position of the allies after D-Day's success in World War II. Talk to a World War II vet of the European Theatre. Like my Dad, they will tell you that it was not a cup of tea after D-Day. The fighting was hard. It was for real. And all of these veterans lost buddies. No, the war wasn't over after D-Day.

And yet historians who study the war tell us that after the success of the invasion, once the Allies had established themselves on the mainland, then Germany had no chance. The war was won or lost on D-Day. The allies were victors. But the war wasn't over. There were still some hard battles to be fought. Blood, sweat, and tears would need to be shed. Lives would be lost. But the final outcome was certain.

My friends, this is the sense in which Jesus is victorious, the sense in which his resurrection has conquered sin, death, and evil. That is the sense in which the heavenly reality of Christ's exaltation like our lesson proclaims speaks to us in our earthy struggles with evil, with doubts, with apathy, and with death. Just like the Allies' eastward march toward the German border was a real struggle, so we are involved in a real struggle with evil and with doubts. It's that struggle that often makes us uncertain and apathetic in our faith. It's a real struggle. And sometimes, like those American soldiers in the war, we will succumb.

In a very real sense, though, the die is cast. Christ *has* conquered. Famed theologian Karl Barth sees this conquest as "the pronouncedly character of his [Christ's] relationship to the orders of life and value current in the world around Him."[92] Elaborating on this point he wrote:

92   Karl Barth, *Church Dogmatics*, Vol.IV/2, eds. G. W. Bromiley and T. F. Torrance, p.171.

... as long as there is history at all [the orders of life and value] enjoy a transitory validity in the history of every human place... This is how he himself deals with them, not in principle, not in the execution of a program, but for this reason in a way which is all the more revolutionary, as the one who breaks all bonds asunder, in new historical developments and situations each of which is for those who can see and hear — only a sign, but an unmistakable sign of his freedom and kingdom and overruling history.[93]

Christ rules over all history. Its values and orders cannot outlast him. There is great comfort in this. Nothing, nothing, nothing but Christ can last forever. The uncertainties, the trials, the moments of despair, they will not last. The business upheavals, the family crises, hassles on the job, international crises, they will not last. Knowing that all these trials will pass makes them a little easier to cope with them. That's the certainty we Christians have. In our struggles with death, evil, uncertainty, and apathy — in all our struggles — we have the assurance that Christ will conquer. We are reassured that the war may not be over yet, but the major battle has been won.

This is the power of the resurrection. It stems from the knowledge and the certainty that on that first Easter, Christ has won the major battle. There is still a war to be fought. We still have to contend with evil. But we cannot lose! How can we be so downhearted about our faith? How can we fail to be enthusiastic about our faith the way we were last Sunday? Why we must be crazy (going against the ways of the world)? In fact, we are on the side of the victor! Facing evil, doubt, and

93   Ibid., p.173.

pain, we rebel against them. Nothing, nothing, nothing, can separate us from the love of God in Christ Jesus. He is victorious!

Christianity: A Worldly Religion That Makes Sure That Even Animals Matter

Christianity is all about salvation — the salvation of our souls, right? That's why the church needs to keep its nose out of politics and all this stuff about polluting the environment. A 2016 Pew Research Center poll found that nearly 1 in 2 of us (47%) feels this way about the church keeping out of politics. And a 2017 poll by Pew found that just over 1 in 2 of us (55%) rank ecological destruction as a major problem. We have had a president who does not want Americans to do much about it (such as Trump's withdrawal from the Paris Accord). Meanwhile, if the most recent US Environmental Protection Agency statistics are to be believed, in 2013 we produced 254 million tons of garbage, so that the average Americans produced 4.4 pounds of disposable stuff a day. We're not improving on those numbers in the past four or five years, have we?

The author of Revelation (said to be John [1:4]) had a vision of the glory of God. And near the end of that vision he looked and tells us:

> ... and I heard the voice of many angels surrounding the throne and the living creatures [the Greek word dzoan is used here, and literally translates "animal"] and the elders; they numbered myriads of myriads and thousands and thousands... (v.11)

Get it? Animals are in heaven, praising God, the Bible says. And then the report of the vision proceeds. In verse 14 it is stated that, "And the four living animals said, 'Amen.'"

Too many preachers fixated on human salvation over the years have missed this point. Our Lord cares about animals, cares about the whole creation! Martin Luther did not miss it. He claimed that Jesus was the Savior of humans and beasts.[94] And he also stated that in heaven there will be nice ponies, that we will be able to handle lions and bears the way we now handle puppies.[95]

It makes sense. Jesus himself is quoted in John (12:47) that he came to save the *world*. And Paul wrote in 2 Corinthians 5:19 that "God was in Christ reconciling the *world* to himself." According to John 12:47, Jesus is reported to have said that he came into the world not to judge the world, but to save it!

God in Christ has come to save the world. He has not just come to save human beings, to save our souls. He came to redeem the whole of creation! God cares so much about the cosmos that he can't bear to have it destroyed. That's probably why animals are in heaven too. They're part of the world that God loves so much that he died for it.

I'm leading up to that unpopular topic that Americans, that American Christians, don't want to hear — ecology. But we have a God Who cares about this

---

94   Martin Luther, "Lectures On 1 Timothy" (1528), in *Luther's Works*, Vol.28, pp.325,326.

95   Martin Luther, Briefwechsel (1530), in D. Martin *Luthers Briefe, Senuschreiben und Bedenken*, Vol.5 (Berlin: Georg Reimer, 1934), p.377; Martin Luther, "Lectures On Genesis" (1535-1538), in *Luther's Works*, Vol. 1, p.65.

matter. He's a God not just interested in spiritual matters — not just concerned with our souls and human beings. God cares about the physical dimensions of the world. He made them too. We have a God Who cares about the plight of the world and its resources. How then can we be indifferent to the plight of the world?

When you understand the Bible, understand the creation story in Genesis in this light, you will begin to appreciate how ecologically concerned the Christian religion is. Think how God makes human beings. He makes us out of the dust of the earth (Genesis 2:6). There's no question about it. According to the Bible, human beings have an intimate connection to the earth. Nature and humanity are intimately related. Without a healthy environment, humanity has no existence.

Oh, but you say that the Bible teaches that we are to subdue the earth, that in Genesis God instruct Adam and Eve to have "dominion over the fish of the sea, and over birds of the air, and over the cattle, and over all the earth..." (Genesis 1:26). "Dominion" implies use, you say. We have authorization here for capitalist economic development.

Not so fast. We need to study the Hebrew language in which the Old Testament was written. You see, the Hebrew word that gets translated "have dominion" in English is *radah*, which literally means "rule." But the Hebrew word *radah* doesn't mean you're a great ruler that everyone bows down to. It's more like being a first among equals. (See Psalm 68:27 where the term is applied to the sense in which the Hebrew tribe of Benjamin, though the smallest of the tribes, is to lead others.)

Yes, that's our status as rulers of the earth. We humans are not given license by God to do whatever we want with the earth and other creatures. We have not been commissioned to exploit it and them. After all, some of them are going to heaven too. They and the whole earth have been saved. No, all the Genesis account in the Bible says is that in relation to the rest of creation, we humans are to be the first among equals. We don't have license to dominate and destroy the earth and all living things. We're only caretakers, guardians, placed on earth to ensure that the word, its creatures, and its resources are developed for their own good and to the glory of God.

There's a beautiful statement issued by the Catholic Church in its Catechism that so nicely makes this point. The statement reads:

> *Man's dominion over inanimate and other living beings granted by the creator is not absolute; it is limited by concern for the quality of life of his neighbor, including generations to come; it requires a religious aspect for the integrity of creation.*[96]

This is not political propaganda. It's just what the Bible says. God loves the world so much that he died for it, so he could restore it, make it new. The book of Revelation says it (21:1). The logic of Christian faith also testifies to the fact that we have a worldly, ecologically sensitive God. Think what happens every Sunday. I recite the Words of Institution (the story of the Last Supper). When I do this, Jesus is present and enters the ordinary bread and wine on our altar. Ordinary bread and wine. Fruits of the earth. But they are certainly not items that are indifferent to our Lord. In fact, he thinks so much of them, they and the earth are so precious to him, that he wraps himself up in them. We have a God

96   *Catechism of the Catholic Church*, 2415.

who actually clothes himself with the physical things of the earth. That's what the Lord's Supper is all about. Christianity is indeed a worldly religion, a faith that affirms that the things of the earth matter.

It's pretty clear. We have a God who loves the things of the earth, who put us humans here to care for it and for all living things.

With a God like we have, who will have animals with him in heaven, who cares for the whole earth and even died for it, a God like that would not seem content with practices that make profit more important than environmental consequences. Would such a God be content with a nation that does not live up to international standards of pollution levels, that lags behind Europe in outlawing gas driven cars? Does a God like that approve of his church's silence on ecological issues?

Please don't hear this sermon as a demand that you get politically involved or boycott businesses that pollute. Just use your common sense on these issues. We don't have a demanding God. No, we have a loving God who loves us so much that he died for us and for his world, for the whole cosmos. Are you grateful for that love? Are you grateful? Then you'll want to care for the physical things of the earth, want to show it the love God's given it and given you.

There is much precedent in the Christian tradition for loving the things God made that way. The founder of the Roman Catholic Franciscan Order of monks and nuns, Francis of Assisi, composed a beautiful song in the middle ages. It went like this:

Praised be thou, my Lord, with all thy creatures,
Especially for Sir Brother Sun...

Praised be thou, my Lord, for Sister Moon and the stars
Formed in the sky, clear, beautiful and fair
Praised be thou, my Lord, for Brother Wind,
For air, for weather cloudy and serene and every weather
By which thou to thy creatures givest sustenance...
Praised be thou, my Lord, for our Mother Earth
Who sustains and rules us
And brings forth divers fruits and coloured flowers and
herbs.[97]

The earth, Francis says, sustains and rules us. Oh how worldly our faith is!

God's intimate relation to the things of the earth entails that we can get to know our Lord a little better through them. Hear the song of the great twentieth-century Catholic theologian Pierre Teilhard de Chardin:

Blessed be you, harsh matter, barren soil, stubborn rock: you who yield only to violence, you who force us to work if we would eat...

Blessed be you, universal matter, immeasurable time, boundless ether, triple abyss of stars and atoms and generations: you who by overflowing and dissolving our narrow standards or measurement reveal to us the dimensions of God...

Blessed be you mortal matter: you who one day will undergo the process of dissolution within us and will thereby take us forcibly into the very heart of that which exists...

---

97   Francis of Assisi, "The Canticle of Brother Sun," in *Readings in Christian Thought,* ed. Hugh Kerr (3rd print.; Nashville, TN: Abingdon Press, 1992), p.101.

You I acclaim as the inexhaustible potentiality for existence and transformation...[98]

All that is depends on God's use of the things of the earth.

As we hear these words of praise for the physical things God has made, a God who forgives us for all the times we forget to care for the creation, we can hear the animals in heaven and the things of the earth sing along with the saints the song of our second lesson. Their song goes like this:

To the one seated on the throne and to the lamb be blessing and honor and glory and might forever and ever. (Revelation 5:13b)

And the animals and the earth sang "Amen." Say it with them now with your new sensitivity to the worldliness of our faith and its ecological sensitivity. Say the Amen with them. Oh it's good to believe in an earthly, worldly religion!

98   Pierre Teilhard de Chardin, *Hymn of the Universe* (New York and Evanston: Harper & Row, 1969), p.69.

Rejoice: Hints Of Heaven Are Here On Earth!

Heaven: Have you ever wondered what it's like? The majority of Americans (72% of us in 2014) believe in heaven, according to a Pew Research poll. Our second lesson from the book of Revelation has some insightful, comforting and refreshing clues. They will shatter our misconceptions as well.

What do you think of heaven? It does not seem to be a very exciting or fun place to be, does it? Oh it seems like a nice place. What could be better than to live in the presence of God? But on the whole, it seems like it could get a little boring there — not much happening. There is not much to do. Everything, it would seem, is so perfect in heaven, that it's not very challenging or exciting to be there. Did you ever feel that way?

The culprit is that we have been too immersed in the philosophy of ancient Greece (the ideas of Socrates and Plato), and not enough immersed in the Bible. Our second lesson can help straighten us out.

You see, ancient Greek philosophy influences us much more than we are aware, even if we don't know much about it and its teachings. To a large extent, Greek philosophy is *the* popular philosophy of Western civilization. We seem instinctively to rely on its basic teachings — like the difference between the body and the soul, its stress on the things of the mind. Its suppositions are tied to the American way of life. And so it interferes with our reading of the Bible.

OK, heaven. What's it like? We can all agree that heaven must be perfect, the perfect place to live. But what is it like to live in a perfect environment? What is perfection? The ancient Greeks taught that what is perfect does not change.[99] Well if that's the case, and if heaven is perfection, then there would not be much to do in heaven. If it's already perfect, and if what is perfect doesn't change, then everything would pretty much stay the same in heaven, nothing new really to do. What do you think?

Anyhow, this is the reason heaven never really seemed all that wonderful to me, and why it seemed so far away. Heaven interpreted in Greek philosophical thinking as unchanging seems a bit inferior to the good things in life as I've experienced it. Sure, the possibility of change causes some problems and anxieties. But the good things in life seem to call you and me to take on new challenges. That's one of the things that makes life so good. In fact, researchers on the human brain have discerned that when undertaking new tasks, the brain forges new neural (brain-cell) connections. When that happens, the front part of our brains (the prefrontal cortex) is saturated with an amphetamine-like, good-feeling brain chemical (dopamine). Doing new things gives you a high.[100]

Suppose we get counter-cultural and rebellious with this Bible lesson. Instead of reading it with Greek philosophical assumptions, let's read it like a Hebrew.

99   Plato, *Parmenides*, 129ff.

100   Sherwin Nuland, *The Art of Aging: A Doctor's Prescription for Well-Being* (New York: Random House, 2008).

Then heaven becomes a more inviting place. And even more exciting, every once-in-a-while, you can even catch a little glimpse of heaven here on earth.

Let's become Hebraic in our thinking. Hebrews (at least those who had not sold out to European domination in the first century) didn't have any of this Greek foolishness about perfection entailing no change. No, for the Hebrews, even God himself changes!

Remember what God's real name is? *Yahweh*. And what does Yahweh mean, what is it derived from? It is derived from the Hebrew phrase "I Am Who I Am," which could also be translated, "I Will Be What I Will Be."[101] Present and future tenses merge in Hebrew at this point. The God of the Hebrews, our God, is future-oriented. He can change and does change (see Genesis 6:6; Exodus 32:14). He is always creating new good. He will not quit that habit in heaven or at the end of time. The Hebrew God does change. What is perfect can change!

Let's now return to our lesson. The author of Revelation had a dream, and in that dream he found himself in heaven. And in heaven, he saw a great multitude which no man could number, faithful from every nation, from all tribes and peoples and tongues, all of them standing before the throne and before the Lamb of God (standing before Jesus Christ). This great crowd was not silent. No, the crowd wasn't silent. It was busy singing praises to God and rejoicing, busy creating new good along with God. Recall, it is God's nature as Yahweh to keep on creating new good. And he will not quit that habit in heaven, as we noted.

---

101 G. W. Anderson, *The History and Religion of Israel* (London: Oxford University Press, 1966), pp.33-34.

Our lesson continues. The author of Revelation notices a special group in the great crowd, those who are clothed in white. He learns that they are martyrs, who died for their faith, or at least they are people who lived out their baptisms and finally killed their old sinful selfish selves for Jesus' sake. Apparently, they have a special job to do in heaven. The serve the Lord day and night, the Bible says (vv.13-15).

The Greek language in which the New Testament was written has at least four different words which can be translated into English as "to serve." The Greek word which appears in our text is the term *latreuo*. It is a term which refers to the kind of service that Jews offer to God while they are worshipping. We're offering that kind of service to God right now, this very moment. The Greek word in our Lesson *latreuo* more or less describes what we are doing here.

That's the point, the main point of this sermon. The saints in heaven, all the faithful in heaven, have something to do. There are activities in heaven. All the citizens of heaven, all those saved at the end of time, we'll all have the task of serving God in worship, or praising him and his Son.

The book of Revelation makes it quite clear. Heaven is not a static and dull place. We'll all be busy in heaven. We'll all be busy here on earth when Christ comes again. We will be busy praising God and rejoicing. We'll be busy creating new good along with God. Our second lesson indicates quite clearly that heaven and life at the end of time are exciting, attractive places to be. We'll have something exciting to do. When you put aside our Greek philosophical prejudices, heaven seems more wonderful to me. How about you? In eternity we are going to have exciting and challenging jobs to do, new challenges, finding ways of assisting God as he keeps on creating new good. What a compelling, powerful way to think about heaven. We'll all be given the privilege of serving the Lord day and night, of finding new opportunities to rejoice and praise him.

Hold on. It gets even better. The heavenly realities are not something far off in the future. No, we have a chance to experience some of them right here and now, or at least to catch glimpses of heaven here on earth. We're doing it just now. Think about this with me.

Our second lesson tells us that in heaven the faithful will serve God in the service that we render when we worship him. We are doing that now. Some of you have even rendered direct service to God in setting up for this worship service. All who have a role in the life of this congregation and the wider church are giving this kind of service. And in offering that service you and I are doing the same sort of thing Peter did in the first lesson (Acts 9:36-43). We are all doing the same sort of thing that the saints in heaven are doing right now, the same sort of thing all of us will be doing at the end of time.

In serving God in this way, in worshiping him like we are now, you and I have a little hints of heaven here on death. We're doing the same thing as the faithful do who have died before us. We have fellowship with them. You and I are not alone. Death hasn't really separated us from our loved ones in the faith. We're all still working together on the same glorious job.

No more can we take worship or the job we have in serving Christ at the church for granted! Because in these activities you and I are on the threshold of heaven, doing what all the dead saints in heaven do, enjoying fellowship with them through participation in a common task. Why what we Christians do in worship and in serving God and our fellow human beings is downright subversive. We have the gall to believe and act like these seemingly flawed human activities get us in touch with eternity! Why you Christians are dangerous in challenging the finiteness, the selfishness, the insignificance of human life that the world teaches us.

Let's get real. Worship or serving God can be dull or painful. What comfort when things get tough. The Protestant Reformer John Calvin said that "there is no surer or more direct course than that which we receive from contempt of the present life and meditation upon heavenly immortality."[102] Martin Luther talked about how a vision of the end time helps us forget the trials on earth.[103] They don't matter so much when you know that all the rottenness before us will wither away, no longer be there to plague us in heaven.

What a glorious vision, what a wonderful view of life this is. When you and I are in worship, doing service to God, then take away all our earthly imperfections, and then you know just a little bit of what heaven's going to be like.

The theme of this Sunday's historic name, *Jubilate* (meaning rejoice) is right on target. Rejoice, people! Rejoice! Even if the world says life and our activities praising and serving God don't matter, we (rebelliously) know better. For we know that hints of heaven are here on earth! That's a good reason to rejoice.

---

102 John Calvin, *Institutes of the Christian Religion*, ed. John T. McNeill, p.722.

103 Martin Luther, "Lectures On Genesis" (1544), in *Luther's Works*, Vol. 7, pp.210,211.

A New Heaven And A New Earth: Our Problems Are Fading Away!

... and God himself will be

with them;
he will wipe away every tear from

their eyes.
death will be no more...
(vv.3-4)

There is not much more that should or could be said about this song in our second lesson. These are compelling images. A God who wants to wipe away every tear from our eyes is a God who you'll want to love. He's a God who makes life a lot easier to live.

If we read these words in light of our whole text for the second lesson, in light of the whole book of Revelation, then the idea of God wiping away tears from our eyes becomes even more comforting. For this is a word of comfort about the whole universe. The text reads:

Then I saw a new heaven and a new earth; for the first heaven and the first earth had passed away. (v.1)

Beautiful, powerful images. But what does it have to do with us, living early in the twenty-first century?

A 2016 Harris poll found that two in three of us are

not very happy in life. As recently as 2016 the National Institute of Mental Health reported that 16.2 million American adults (6.7% of us) suffer from depression. So many of us, even those of us not struggling with depression and unhappiness, feel boxed in, burned out. Often, we feel trapped by our circumstances, living with a sense of hopelessness. We clearly are people who need a fresh start, who need a God who will wipe away all our tears and overcome death.

Before addressing these issues, I want to call you attention to how the reference in verse 4 of our lesson to God overcoming death seems to be a deliberate reference to Isaiah 25:8 which reads:

He will swallow up death forever, and the Lord will wipe away tears from all faces.

Indeed Revelation frequently quotes other Old Testament texts. A lot of its ideas come from the book of Daniel.[104]

The links between the Old and New Testaments that Revelation and our second lesson posit entail that we have to understand the links between the testaments in the context of the whole sweep of human history, from the creation of the universe to the day Revelation was written in the late first century to today. We have in the second lesson and in the book of Revelation as a whole a testimony about God's plan for the *totality* of human history. God's overcoming of death and wiping away our tears is a universal, trans-historical event.

What does all this have to do with the unhappiness, depression, and burn-out with which many of us wrestle? Our lesson is teaching us that the comfort that

104 See Revelation 11:7/Daniel 7:3,7,21; Revelation 12:7/Daniel 10:13,21; 12:1; Revelation 20:1,4/Daniel 7:9,22,27.

God gives is part of his universal project of making all things new, and that puts our anxiety, unhappiness, and worries in perspective. The comfort God gives entails that his overcoming death and drying our tears are part of his worldwide, universal aims!

The spiritual founder of Methodism John Wesley spoke of the cosmic character of the change God's comfort makes. He wrote:

As there will be no more death and no more pain or sickness preparatory thereto; as there will be no more sorrow or crying. Nay, but there will be a greater deliverance than all this; for there will be no more sin. And to crown all, there will be a deep, an intimate, an uninterrupted union with God... a continual enjoyment of the Three-One God, and all creatures in him![105]

When we consider the great things God is doing, actually putting an end to all death, all conflict, the problems and anxieties and fears you and I encounter are not such a big deal after all. My fears, your problems and anxieties, get swallowed up, overwhelmed by God's cosmic, universal, repair and re-creation job. They are all overcome, they all get lost in the deep, intimate, uninterrupted union with God to which John Wesley was referring. If God is abolishing death, all evil, all conflict, wrapping all the faithful up in an intimacy with him, what chance does anxiety about a job, about a fight with a spouse, about burn-out or lack of self-confidence have?

The book of Revelation was written at a time when the Christians to whom it was written were suffering persecution from the Roman Empire. The message of

---

105 John Wesley, "Sermons," in *The Works of John Wesley, Vol.6* (3ʳᵈ ed.; Grand Rapids, MI: Baker, 1996), p.296.

the book was that these persecutions are not the real crisis facing the world. The real crisis is God's activity purging the world of all sin and evil, making it new! Likewise, today the real crisis is not our economic uncertainties, nuclear holocaust, global warming, or terrorism. The real crisis is not our personal anxiety. No, the real crisis is the absolute certainty that God is coming to judge the world, make it new, and that as he does this he'll be wiping away every tear from our eyes.

Speaking of crises, famed twentieth-century theologian Karl Barth had an important insight. In the spirit of Chicago Mayer Rahm Emmanuel who claimed that "crises are something you don't want to waste" (a point made while he was President Obama's Chief of Staff), Barth contended that crises are good for faith. Crises are good for faith, he claimed, because if you are not fully engaged in something it does not matter, and then we begin to take it for granted.[106]

Barth helps us better understand this crisis too. The real crisis is not the persecution of first-century Christians. It is not global warming, the Trump presidency, or our own ups and downs. The real crisis is that the universe is under judgment because it is finite, and it must pass away, and that God is coming in Christ in the midst of it all to give us a fresh start![107]

Our second lesson and the book of Revelation point us toward a new way of looking at our faith, at our lives, to look at it all from a cosmological, universal perspective. They remind us that the significance of Christ's work needs to be interpreted in light of God's

---

106 Karl Barth, *Epistle to the Romans*, trans. Edwyn Hoskyns (London and New York: Oxford University Press, 1933), pp.32,39-40,91.

107 Ibid., p.77.

concern to redeem the whole world, the whole universe. Likewise our lives and our circumstances need to be interpreted in that light, in light of God's concern to redeem the whole world, the universe. From that point of view, God is tearing us away from ourselves, tearing us away from the petty personal anxieties, form the latest trend, tearing us away from your personal hang-ups so we're really free to recognize that God has in a sense already begun creating the new heaven and the new earth. In so doing God makes it possible to begin to see the new thing he is creating, setting out to wipe every tear from our eyes.

When you have been set free from yourself in this way, set free from your hang-ups and from the latest cultural trends, when you have been cut loose from yourself and set adrift in the majesty and splendor of the whole universe that God has been redeeming, then your little problems and despair, the latest trends won't count so much to you anymore. When all those problems and griefs don't count so much, that's God wiping away those tears from your eyes.

When you're lost in God's majesty, engaged in an uninterrupted union with him (like John Wesley advocated), when you realize your place in the new heaven and the new earth, then all your problems start fading away. What chance do they have in face of such love, with a God who makes all things new (v.5)? No, praise God, they all fade away!

Christian: Don't Get So Hung Up On Churchy Things!

In the Spirit [one of the seven angels] carried me away to a great, high mountain, and showed me the holy city Jerusalem coming down out of heaven from God...

And I saw no temple in the city, for its temple is the Lord God the Almighty and the lamb. And the city has no need of sun or moon to shine upon it, for the glory of God is its light, and its lamp is the lamb. (21:10,22-23)

There was no temple in the city. Heaven is a place without a temple.

A Barna Poll in 2016 found while 73% of Americans identify themselves as Christians, only 37% are likely to be in church (and people typically lie about church attendance in polls).

A 2016 Pew Research Center poll found that 20% of the religiously unaffiliated are turned off by institutional religion. It's all about being "spiritual," not "religious," it seems.

This vision of the New Jerusalem at the end of time that the writer of the book of Revelation had has a lot to do with life for us today. The connection has to do with the fact that God has become incarnate in Jesus Christ.

The Incarnation: What do we mean when we talk about the Incarnation? First and foremost, the Incarnation refers to the fact that in the man Jesus, God has taken on human flesh. God is found in earthly things. (Preachers believing in Christ's real presence in the Lord's Supper might also add how the church believes that God s actually *in* the bread and wine.) We even believe that God is present in our church buildings when we gather around the altar to worship him. A God who became incarnate in Jesus still becomes incarnate in earthly things today.

Historically, one of the reasons that church buildings have been considered special, even holy, is related to Christianity's incarnation emphasis. But it is also related to Christianity's roots in Judaism. Recall that the ancient Hebrews believed that Yahweh lived in the Jerusalem temple (2 Chronicles 7:1; 1 Kings 9:3). This is what makes our lesson all the more striking, when we are told that there will be no temple in the New Jerusalem. There will be no temple there, for its temple is the Lord God.

The point of this vision seems to be that we are worship God spiritually. In our gospel lesson for today, Jesus promises to send the Spirit (John 14:26). God is Spirit! John Calvin made this point nicely: "For God is incomprehensible, a Spirit above all spirit, light above all light."[108]

Famed twentieth-century theologian Paul Tillich defined "Spirit" as that which includes all that is in a unity, but a unity with a purpose. In that sense, he claimed, God is Spirit.[109]

108 John Calvin, "The Clear Explanation of Sound Doctrine Concerning the True Partaking of the Flesh and Blood of Christ in the Holy Supper" (1561), in *Calvin: Theological Treatises*, ed. J.K.S. Reid (Philadelphia: Westminster, 1965), p.302.

109 Paul Tillich, *Systematic Theology*, Vol.1 (3 vols. in 1; Chicago: University of Chicago Press, 1967), p.249.

Calvin and Tillich agree. As Spirit, God is not unduly attached to anything earthly. That's why we can't ever fully know him, Calvin contends. And if he was attached especially to something earthly, God could not be what unifies everything, Tillich adds, "Consequently, the religiously unaffiliated are correct up to a point. God is not just about religions and their activities!"

Because God is Spirit, worship needs to be spiritual, not unduly attached to visible means like a church building, a favorite preacher, or particular church activities. We should not forget the Incarnation, that God became incarnate. But we need to seek to worship the way we will in heaven, the way we will at the end of time. And that means seeking to worship God spiritually, not just through his incarnate means.

This seems like a contradiction: On one hand contending that God is linked to earthly things (as incarnate) and also maintaining freedom from these things. And what is the significance of all this for our daily lives and our walk of faith?

Christian faith involves a balancing act. Here on earth the faithful need to seek the golden mean between extremes. We Christians do that with the Trinity, saying that God is three but also one. However, you can't stress his threeness to the point that God's unity is compromised and you wind up with three gods. And you can't stress his unity to the point that no real distinction is made between the three persons. You have to have it both ways.

Same with the idea that Christ is both divine and human, but still one. You want to keep those two natures of Jesus distinct. But you can't stress that so much that you wind up with two different people living inside Jesus' body. The unity of Jesus' person must be protected, but not to the point of abolishing the distinctions between his divine and human natures.

So it is with God's presence: We need the "golden" mean here too. We need to find a way to affirm both the spirituality of (defying his absolute identification with anything that is institutional and physical) and also the incarnational nature of our Lord. We want to affirm his presence in Christ, in the church, in the Bible, in preaching, and in worship. But we also want to affirm with the dream reported on in our lesson that God is more than the visible means he uses, that he is a God who needs no sun or moon because his very presence lights up the heavens and the earth. Before such a God all our words, good deeds, church programs, church buildings, and ideas melt away into insignificance. We want to affirm a God not bound by ecclesiastical institution and not too churchy.

Now don't get me wrong in all this. I'm not suggesting that the way to the Christian life involves rejection of the Incarnation, the ignoring of the sacraments, of preaching, and of church life in order to attain true spirituality and the knowledge of God. No, I'm saying just the opposite, that we need to keep the emphasis on the Incarnation, we need to continue to venerate and respect the visible and creaturely entities through which God reveals himself. There is nothing wrong with respect for church buildings, veneration of the sacraments, and the sermon. Certainly there is nothing wrong with our commitments to and enthusiasm for programs and other work in our congregation and the wider church. The only thing is that these must be kept in the proper perspective, in a creative tension that God portrayed in our second lesson, the God whose majesty requires no temple, whose very presence lights up the heavens and the earth.

It is good that God became incarnate and still reveals himself incarnationally. This is his way of making every realm in life his business, of taking away our excuse that he is not present in every sphere of our lives. This takes away our excuses for not worshiping, because an Incarnate God is present in the ordinary things of life, including our singing and liturgy.

The problem, you see, is not with God's incarnational propensities but our sinful condition louses things up, our propensity to take creatures and make them our gods. We make our own gods, Martin Luther said, when we put our trust in some physical entity or value.[110] Too often we are guilty of making money, pleasure, power, or our jobs, even our families and church programs our gods.

Our second lesson and its picture of the God who needs no temple calls us away from undue fascination with our church buildings. If the majority of church's time and energy is devoted to questions about property and our programs, if it's easier to get people to meetings and fellowship events than to study the scriptures in a disciplined way, then something's wrong, and the religiously unaffiliated are right to call us to task. Then we're forgetting our second lesson and its picture of the God who needs no temple.

Our lesson calls us away from idolatry; it calls us to spiritual worship of God, to seek more experience of the presence of God who needs no temple, whose

110   Martin Luther, "The Large Catechism" (1529), in *The Book of Concord*, eds. Robert Kolb and Timothy Wengert, 386.

glory lights up the world and our lives. This kind of spirituality, faith that puts spiritual development, Bible reading, and prayer at the center of our activities, this sort of spirituality is what it will take to make us a vibrant congregation — a spirituality that can attract the millennials and the religiously unaffiliated.

Let us continue to celebrate God's Incarnation in our buildings, in our programs, in our organizations, and in our fellowship. But let us not forget that all these must diminish, must take second place in our lives and in the commitments and activities of our church, second place to the God of our second lesson who does not need these things.

Next time you feel drawn away from spirituality, too busy to pray, to contemplate God's mysteries, too caught up in the accumulation of wealth, influence, power, even church programs, remember the vision of this second lesson. The Incarnate God is present in the most ordinary earthly things you are now encountering. God does not need those things; his glory and presence far outweigh the earthly activities in which we are engaged. Nothing that has been created (even church activities) can ultimately compete with the magnificent, loving God into whose presence we have come. Oh how good and glorious it is to be in the presence of God!

The Triumph Of God's Grace

God put this power to work in Christ when he raised him from the dead and seated him at his right hand in the heavenly places; far above all rule and authority and power and dominion, and above every name that is named, not only in this age but also in the age to come. And he has put all things under his feet... (vv.20-22a)

God's power is at work in both the resurrection and in today's miracle — the Ascension. Everything has been put under Christ. Everything!

So what? In the Ascension we see God in all his glory! This is a glory overflowing with love. The sixteenth-century Protestant Reformer John Calvin nicely developed this point. He says that the Ascension helps us appreciate grace even more, helps make us sure that we not be cast down by our own unworthiness. He wrote:

Paul's object was not only to impress the Ephesians with a deep sense of the value of divine grace, but also to give them exalted views of the glory of Christ's kingdom. That they might not be cast down by a view of their own unworthiness, he exhorts them to consider the power of

God; as if he had said that their regeneration was no ordinary work of God, but was an astonishing exhibition of his power.[111]

To this Calvin adds that Christ is a mirror of the glorious treasure of grace.[112]

Nice sentiments. But a lot of Americans, nearly half of us, do not believe these words. A 2008 Baylor University poll indicated that nearly one of two Americans believe in a judgmental God.[113]

Americans caught up in this vision of God are inevitably unhappy, ever fretful that their own lives don't measure up and will in the end get the punishment they deserve for shortcomings. All of us die someday, have lost loved ones, and have had disappointments. When you have a judgmental God, all these experiences count as punishments for a life not well lived.

Even for those of us not caught up in the idea of an angry God, without assurance that grace ultimately triumphs, life is still full of despair. Famed French intellectual Blaise Pascal described such an outlook on life so poignantly:

I see the terrifying spaces of the universe hemming me in, and I find myself attached to one corner of this vast experience without knowing why I have been put in this place rather than that, or why the brief span of life allotted to me should be assigned to one moment rather than another of all the eternity that went before me and will come after me. I see only infinity on every side hemming

---

111   John Calvin, *Calvin's Commentaries*, Vol.XXI/1 (reprint ed.; Grand Rapids, MI: Baker Books, 2005), p.214.

112   Ibid., p.215.

113   Paul Froese and Christopher Bader, *America's Four Gods* (New York and Oxford: Oxford University Press, 2010).

me in like an atom or like the shadow of a fleeting in-
stant. All I know is that I must soon die, but what I know
least about is this very death which I cannot evade.[114]

We have no meaning in life as long as eternity and infinity are not friendly toward us. If we have nothing in our past but meaningless busyness, nothing right now but blind chance, nothing up ahead but annihilation there is no meaning.

Another French intellectual, the existentialist Albert Camus described the life of despair just as forcefully. He said that despair is accepting your condition even when you can't stand it.[115] Famed German-American theologian Paul Tillich put it this way:

The pain of despair is the agony of being responsible for
the loss of meaning of one's existence and of being unable
to recover it. One is shut up in one's self and in the con-
flict with one's self.[116]

The Ascension story helps take away this despair. For in the Ascension, Jesus the man and the God of love returned to the Father. The one Who died for us is also the Word of God who created the universe (John 1)! God's love or grace is the glue that holds the created order together. Our second lesson today claims that all things are under our Lord Christ's feet (v.22).

Martin Luther King, Jr. nicely made this point regarding how the love of God (he believed that to be Christ) is the creative force of the universe:

114 Blaise Pascal, *Pensees*, trans. A. J. Krailsheimer (Middlesex, UK: Penguin, 1966), p.158.

115 Albert Camus, *The Rebel*, trans. Anthony Bower (3 vols. in 1; Chicago: University of Chicago Press, 1967), p.14.

116 Paul Tillich, *Systematic Theology*, Vol.2, p.75.

Whether we call it an unconscious process, an impersonal Brahman, or a personal being of matchless power and infinite love, there is a creative force in this universe that works to bring the disconnected aspects of reality into a harmonious whole.[117]

A writer named Eric Collier offers a thoughtful elaboration on this point. He has stated:

God's power, glory, and majesty makes me feel like I don't deserve to be in the same room with him. His love, mercy, and compassion lets me know I don't belong anywhere else.

Yes, God is awesome. So is his Son now in heaven. We do not deserve his love and grace. But where else is there is a safe place to go, what with all the death and despair that surround us?

To be sure, death and meaninglessness still surround us. But ultimately they cannot win! Christ's Ascension assures us that he has overcome them all. The Dutch heroine of the Holocaust, Corrie ten Boom, powerfully described the outcome of the Ascension. It provides a word of hope while we despair over God's rule in the world, despair over the growing apparent irrelevance of life, despair over the direction of our own lives. Her word of hope was that "No matter how deep our darkness — he is deeper still."

No matter how low we go, Christ is there. The Ascension entails that in the church, in the world, we are never alone. Where God is, there is Jesus and his guiding, unifying love!

---

117 Martin Luther King, Jr., Stride Toward Freedom: The Montgomery Circle (1958), in *A Testament of Hope: The Essential Writings of Martin Luther King, Jr.*, ed. James M. Washington (San Francisco, Harper & Row, 1986), p.20.

Christ is in heaven! His Ascension means that this love governs the universe. The grace-filled presence of God is everywhere, higher than the heights, deeper than the depths, more inside the heart, and yet enveloping all that is beyond us. Death, meaninglessness, despair, and a sense that we cannot recover from them are gone. They do not have a chance in face of Christ, who now embodies the cosmic character of grace.

Famed modern theologian Karl Barth nicely explained the meaning of Christ's Ascension and its significance in this spirit:

> *What is the meaning of the Ascension? According to what we have said about heaven and earth, it means at any rate that Jesus leavens earthly space, the space, that is, which is conceivable to us... He stands above the space, he fulfills it and he becomes present to it... Our flesh, our human nature is exalted above in him to God. The end of his work is that we are with him above. We with him beside God.*[118]

The next time death, meaninglessness, boredom, despair, and a sense that we cannot recover from them creep into your life, remember how when Christ ascended he took you and me (at least the human nature we share with him) along with him to God's side. This is a God who is not judgmental, but a God who is full of grace and love for you and me. Then you'll truly appreciate why sadness and meaningless don't have a chance. For the Ascension of Jesus reminds us that contrary to what the world tells us, life in the world has meaning and is filled with God's love — precisely because Jesus is right there at God's side, ever reminding the Father how much he loves human beings like you

118 Karl Barth, *Dogmatics in Outline* (New York: Harper & Row, 1959), p.125.

and me. This love is now the very force that permeates the cosmos and so saturates your life and more.

Easter 7
Revelation 22:12-14,16-17,20-21

Life Between The Times

Famed twentieth-century theologian Karl Barth has claimed that this text, in which Jesus promises to be coming soon (vv.12,20), testifies to a present that looks back to Jesus and expects his final revelation. All time is the time of the man Jesus:

> *Can the Christianity and the church that really derive and are grounded in the resurrection of Jesus Christ ever be anything better than the place where, from out of and beyond all the required representations of Jesus Christ, the kingdom, the covenant, reconciliation and its fruit, men can only cry and call out: "Lord, have mercy upon us! Even so, come Lord Jesus?" Is not perhaps the surest test of genuine Christianity and church life whether the men united in it exist wholly in this expectation and therefore not at all in a supposed present possession of the glorious presence of their Lord?[119]*

So what? The theme of this final Sunday of the Easter Season is that we live in the time of Jesus, the time between his resurrection and his second coming. What difference does it make? Understanding life as a living between the times or eras entails that life is to be lived with expectancy. Are you living that way? Or is tomorrow just another day, the coming work-week just

119 Karl Barth, *Church Dogmatics, Vol.IV/3*, Pt.1, trans. G. W. Bromiley (Edinburgh: T. & T. Clark, 1961), p.322.

more days on the job, this afternoon's family lunch just another meal?

When you live your life as between the times, dedicated to Jesus, seeing the present as his time too, then it puts you in tension with the ordinary humdrum way of living. Nobody gets bored when they live between the times of Jesus. Everything is urgent. Any minute he could come! In the best sense this is a life lived on the edge.

The eminent New Testament scholar Rudolf Bultmann nicely explains the urgency associated with living with an eye towards expectation about the future. He wrote:

> *This is the deeper meaning of the mythological preaching of Jesus — to be open to God's future which is really imminent for every one of us: to be prepared for this future which comes as a thief in the night when we do not expect it; to be prepared because this future will be judgment on all men who have bound themselves to the world and are not free, not open to God's future.*[120]

Martin Luther King operated with a similar viewpoint, as he stated, "We are now faced with the fact my friends that tomorrow is today. We are confronted with the fierce urgency of now."[121] It is like the inventor of the electric starter Charles Kettering once said: "My interest is in the future because I am going to spend the rest of my life there."[122]

120 Rudolf Bultmann, *Jesus Christ and Mythology* (New York: Charles Scribner's Sons, 1958), pp.31-32.

121 Martin Luther King, Jr., *A Call to Conscience: The Landmark Speeches of Martin Luther King, Jr.*, ed. Clayborne Carson (New York: Warner Books, 2008), p.162.

122 Charles Kettering, "Testimonial Dinner Speech To Chamber of Commerce," Lansing, MI, 1938.

Modern theology has gotten interested in this idea of life being lived with an awareness of being between times, lived with the future in view. One of the great proponents of this way of thinking is a German theologian names Jurgen Moltmann. On this matter he has written:

"Christianity" has its essence and is good not in itself and not in its own existence, but lives from something and exists for something that reaches far beyond itself... If we would fathom its essence then we must enquire into that future on which it sets its hopes and expectations.[123]

A lot like Martin Luther King Jr. and the Black church in America, Moltmann goes on to say that when you have a mission for the future, when you have the dream inspired by God and his kingdom, it gives you the kind of hope you need to have the courage to seek justice. You can live with the setbacks, take the risks you need to on the way to justice, because you know that justice is a future reality that's coming.[124]

A life lived with this kind of hope, with confidence that the future is in God's hands, is also a life full of joy. Nineteenth-century German writer Johann von Goethe made that point profoundly in a poem:

Why go chasing distant fancies?
Lo, the good is ever near!
Only learn to grasp your changes!
Happiness is always here.[125]

---

123 Jurgen Moltmann, *Theology of Hope*, trans. James Leitch (New York and Evanston: Harper & Row, 1967), p.325.

124 Ibid., p.338; Martin Luther King Jr., "I Have a Dream," (Washington, DC, 1963).

125 Johann von Goethe, as quoted in Ibid., p.27.

We have previously noted that there is sound scientific evidence for this observation about the benefits of living with openness to and confidence in the future. When you do that it seems that the brain is forging new brain-cell connections, and when that happens our brains reward us by secreting an amphetamine-like brain chemical, dopamine, which is pleasurable, makes you happy and enhances energy.[126] A believer living between the times will rebel against all the meaninglessness and boredom of life, find joy and be filled with energy to take on the tasks of everyday life. In his play titled *Landscape of the Body*, playright John Guare offers a line which expresses these same sentiments: "It is amazing how a little tomorrow [he writes] can make up for a whole lot of yesterday." With Jesus and his kingdom in your future a lot of yesterday (filled with all the disappointments, mistakes, and regrets) no longer matters.

When you live between the times, and understand it all as the time of the man Jesus, then you live with more joy than someone just stuck in the present, because the future is in view, and you also live with Jesus and his past. That means that like we heard Karl Barth say at the beginning of this sermon, all time belongs to Jesus. With a lifestyle like that you are never alone, always with Jesus and his heritage as well as with his future in view. When you see yourself as living between the times (the time between Jesus on earth and his second coming), then all history, and so your whole life has been surrounded by Jesus and his love

---

126 Sherwin Nuland, *The Art of Aging: A Doctor's Prescription for Well-Being*; Daniel Amen, *Change Your Brain, Change Your Life* (New York: Three Rivers, 1998), p.81.

for you. With the present, future, and past all held together, Christians can live like early twentieth-century American journalist William Allen White once said: "I am not afraid of tomorrow, for I have seen yesterday and I live today."

We have already talked about Rudolf Bultmann (the great New Testament scholar). He also says that a faith that has you living between times calls you away from yourself and the ways of the world. In that sense it's a rebellious lifestyle. He wrote:

> *It is the word of God which calls man away from his selfishness and from the illusory security he has built up for himself... Faith is the abandonment of man's own security and the readiness to find security only in the unseen beyond, in God. This means that faith is security where no security can be seen; it is as Luther said, the readiness to enter confidently into the darkness of the future. Faith in God Who has power over time and eternity, and who calls me and who has acted new is acting on me — this faith can become real only in its "nevertheless" against the world.*[127]

In faith we submit to the God who is in control of, is present, through all time. For Christians living between the times, yesterday and today are good, filled with Jesus, and the end looks even better. This gives us the courage to move with confidence into the glorious future God has planned. What a blessing it is that Jesus has elected to live and to let us live in this time!

---

127 Rudolf Bultmann, *Jesus Christ and Mythology* (New York: Charles Scribner's Sons, 1958), pp.40-41.